ARRIVING

Freedom Writings by
Asian and Pacific Islanders Behind and Beyond Bars

Compiled by
Asian Prisoner Support Committee

Cover Illustration & Book Design by Don Aguillo

Printed in the United States of America

First Printing: 2024
Published by Eastwind Books
2022 University Avenue, Box 46
Berkeley, CA 94704

www.AsiaBookCenter.com
Email: eastwindbooks@gmail.com

ISBN: 9781961562011 (Paperback)
ISBN: 9781961562028 (Ebook)

Contents

Foreword   i
Thi Bui

Introduction   iii
Nathaniel Tan

War   1

Haunted   2
Phoeun You

New   7
Kamsan Suon

Fish Out of Water   9
Hieu "Rocky" Nguyen

Video Vault Unlocked   14
Hung T. Ly

Memory   18

My Name   20
Kamsan Suon

My His-Story: Growing Up A Half Breed in the USA   21
John V. Apollo

American Dream   26
Remus James Langi

Running   28
Vu Bui

Resentment & Forgiveness   36
Si Dang

From Growing Up to Growing Pains   43
Saiyez Ahmed

White World   46
Kamsan Suon

Within Prison   **50**

Open Eyes   51
Billy Gumabon

Asian Shame - An American Stain   53
Franklin Lee

SHU   58
Tautai Seumanu Jr.

The Non-Designation Paradox   60
Douglas Yim

Voice of the Voiceless   67
Ricky May

Organizing for Freedom: An Interview with Charles "Bula" Joseph   69

Outside/Inside Power   77
Adamu Chan

R.O.O.T.S.   82
Rhummanee Hang

Beyond Prison   **86**

Captured Moments   87
Tautai Seumanu Jr.

Something in Common We Trust   91
Michael Manjeet Singh

Fighting the Power   95
Michael Manjeet Singh

From Surviving Systemic Violence to Liberating People from Prisons and ICE Detentions   96
Ny Nourn

The Awakening   103
Bao Vu Nguyen

Spiritual Quest   106
Nou Phang Thao

Healing   114

Spinning with the Earth   115
Kenny Lee

Lost & Found   116
Kenny Lee

Thou Shall Not Judge   125
Ricky May

Unveiling the Curtains   127
Tien N. Nguyen

Lost Dream / "Path of Hope"   135
Chandra Kishor

The Chronicles of Hung T. Ly   137
Hung T. Ly

Circles   145
John Lam

When We Fight, We Win: An Interview With Kanley Souetpich   148

Bike Work as Self Work: An Interview with Ke Lam   152

Me & My Brother   156
Maria "Kanaka" Luna

Home   159

Longing for Home...   162
Ung Bang

Motherland   165
Bao Vu Nguyen

For My People   167
Michael Manjeet Singh

Formosa   168
Tien-Hsiang Mo

Letter to Abuela   170
Eusebio Gonzalez

Fishing Trip: An Interview With Chanthon Bun and Trung Tong   175

Afterword   **180**
Eddy Zheng

Acknowledgements   **183**

About the Contributors   **185**

About Asian Prisoner Support Committee   **195**

**Other Works By Asian Prisoner Support
Committee**   **196**

Foreword
Thi Bui

I cannot help but write from the vantage point of who I am, so let me state that I am an educated professional who has never been behind bars; I am also a refugee from Viet Nam and, equally relevant here, I am a parent. A mother who has earned her gray hairs caring for a child from the womb to early adulthood.

Why do we care for our young? It's not just to keep them alive. Everything we do is motivated in some way by the fear of what will happen if we don't do it. If I don't make sure x then y will happen. He'll grow up without the skills to make a happy life. He'll miss out on x.

What happens to our young people when families are not able to provide all the necessary things to survive and thrive? When external forces are too great? Bombs falling from American airplanes. Political upheaval. Genocide. Reeducation camps. Refugee camps. Resettlement into strange new cities with their own poverty and violence. Drugs. Alcoholism. Domestic violence. Mental illness. How are young seedlings with no roots to thrive in these conditions? How can they even survive, except by becoming hard? And at what cost?

There is an urgent need expressed by many of these writers to be seen in the full spectrum of their humanity. There is a longstanding and pervasive disregard for Asian people in American culture, which anti-Asian attacks during the pandemic have forced into current public discourse. Against the erasure of Asian Americans and Pacific Islanders in this country, many of us have cried out in myriad ways, "We are here. We are here. We are here."

But we have far to go in our conception of who WE are. I am calling out my fellow educated professionals. My model minorities and exceptional refugees. My pearl-clutching, trauma-suffering brethren: I love you, and also you need to embrace our complexity.

Why should we care for the incarcerated and formerly incarcerated? Because *not my problem* is not only terrible policy, it's a fallacy. In the words of Angela Davis, "Prisons do not disappear social problems, they disappear human beings. Homelessness, unemployment, drug addiction, mental illness, and illiteracy are only a few of the problems that disappear from public view when the human beings contending with them are relegated to cages." Prisons break up families. Prisons create new problems. They have not made this country safer.

But don't let just someone like me tell you this. Hear it from the people who live it, have survived it, have something to say about it. Reader, they have hope! And so much fight. If someone who has been locked up for years without the possibility of parole has hope for humanity and a light still shining in them, I think they are better fit to lead us out of this vicious cycle of suffering than those who prey on our fears to build more walls, more prisons, more bombs.

We have much to do as a society to make things right. One big step is listening to the people most impacted by the things society has gotten wrong. There is no one voice that can represent all AAPIs who have been incarcerated. Thank goodness there is this anthology of many voices. I'm so excited for you to read these stories, to share them, teach them, heal with them, and change the world with them.

Thi Bui
Author of *The Best We Could Do*

Introduction
Nathaniel Tan

In the past few decades, there has been a steady rise in the incarceration of Asian and Pacific Islanders (API), specifically Southeast Asians and Pacific Islanders. The general discourse around APIs in prison have been close to nonexistent. APIs are invisibilized in the discussion of mass incarceration and mass deportation.

What is commonly understood is that the "school-to-prison pipeline" has been the lexicon to describe the funneling of young people into America's criminal legal system. This pipeline does not include the experiences of APIs. Due to war, U.S. imperialism, and America's deep seated xenophobia, APIs go through a pipeline best described as the migration-to-school- to-prison-to-deportation pipeline with Southeast Asians and Pacific Islanders making up the majority of this pipeline's subjects.

This anthology captures the lived experiences of incarcerated APIs in prison in hopes of bringing broader attention to this social injustice faced by APIs. We believe that these stories shed light on this pipeline, expose it, and interrupt it.

However, shedding light on this issue is not enough. It is crucial that we take action to address the systemic racism and oppression that API communities face in the criminal legal system. We must push for policies and reforms that prioritize rehabilitation and reintegration instead of punishment and exclusion. We must also work to change the narrative around APIs in the media and public discourse, recognizing the unique struggles and experiences they face.

We hope this anthology will heal, inspire, and empower readers to take action, make change, and build solidarity with people impacted by the carceral system.

•••

> "No one of us can be free until everybody is free."
> Maya Angelou

WAR

Art by
Chanthon Bun

Haunted
Phoeun You

Early one morning, Puma woke to the sound of thunderous explosions, like old Western war movies. The earth rattled as bombs were dropped on his village. Thick smoke formed, and flames filled the air. Bamboo huts that were sitting on stilts burned and crumbled to the ground. Debris came down like a hailstorm. Outside, Puma saw mothers running out of their homes carrying babies in their arms as they scattered for safety. He witnessed children running and crying frantically as they searched for their parents.

Born in Cambodia on December 7, 1975, Puma was the second youngest of ten siblings: six sisters and three brothers. He was born in an era when many Cambodians lost loved ones by execution, an era in which the Khmer Rouge regime implemented ethnic cleansing to keep Cambodians "pure." Before the rise of the Khmer Rouge regime, Puma's father had been a doctor at a local clinic. His mother had been a homemaker. After their village was bombed, Puma and his family were forced to leave their home behind.

Puma and his family walked for four days in the scorching hot sun. The sun made Puma dazed, thirsty, and tired. The dry heat caused his mouth to become sticky, and his saliva felt like strings of yarn. On the side of the road were other families fleeing the Khmer Rouge soldiers. They reminded him of army ants, marching with large bundles of supplies along a dirt road. Puma's feet ached from the burning hot dirt road. When he got too tired, his dad tied a red sarong across his shoulder and carried Puma in a sling on his back. "It's okay," his father reassured him. "Don't be scared. I'll take care of you."

From the sarong, Puma saw people sleeping on the side of the road. Some lay still and didn't move. As he passed by, he saw families resting and eating under a shaded tree, a mother breastfeeding her newborn. For those who were frozen on the road, he wondered if they were dead. They had a yellow complexion, their mouths open.

•••

To get to Thailand, Puma and his family crossed the Mekong River, where he witnessed bodies floating with the current.

"Don't stare at the bodies. Their spirits will come and haunt you," Puma's dad said.

Puma was cautious when he passed through the dark jungles of Cambodia. The tall grass did not allow for a clear visual, and the quiet made Puma feel as if someone or something could be lurking in the bushes. The air was cool, and the only sound he heard was rustling leaves. Or were they the echoes of howling ghosts hovering above the jungles? Puma's father had told him that ghosts lingered in the forest—evil spirits who hadn't been accepted on the other side. The sounds of the jungle sent cold chills up Puma's spine and caused the hair on his arms to rise.

Later that day, Puma was stricken with stomach pains. "Dad, my tummy hurts," he said. Tears trickled down his face. "I'm sorry, Son—I have to portion the food for everyone. There's plenty of food where we're going." His father pointed into the trees. "Go use the bathroom. It'll make you feel better."

Puma entered the forest and searched for a secluded area behind tall grass to release the pressure in his belly. He walked slowly and carefully into the bushes. Once he located a spot, Puma crouched down. From this position, he noticed a swarm of flies behind another patch of tall grass. The smell of rotten fish lingered in the air. It reminded him of the fishing season, when villagers would salt fish and leave them out to dry in the sun.

Puma grabbed a long branch on the ground next to his feet. He used it to part the grass for a better visual. The swarm of vibrating flies guided the direction of his stick. Puma probed and poked with the branch until he detected something stiff on the ground. The stiffness felt like an animal. Using the stick as his fingers, he could feel its firm muscle. And beneath the flesh he could feel something hard, like bones or ribs.

Puma stood. At first, he couldn't make out what he saw. He thought it might be a large dog with black fur. The more he inspected, the more was revealed. What he thought was fur was actually long, black hair. Puma used the twig to rake the hair aside, exposing a woman's face. Yellow, puffy, with swollen eyes and purple lips. Maggots crawled out of her nose and mouth. Puma's eyes widened; his heart beat faster. The woman lay on her stomach with her head tilted to the side. She wore a skirt hiked to her waist, revealing slightly separated legs. The smell was horrific. The flies buzzed and hovered around the carcass. Puma stood there with his mouth gaping, staring at the corpse.

"Hurry up! We got to go!" Puma's father shouted into the forest. His voice made Puma blink, breaking his trance. He ran back to the safety of his father's protection. Afraid to be reminded of the dead woman's body, Puma never mentioned it to his father and remained silent the rest of the way.

•••

After two weeks, Puma and his family arrived at their destination: Sa Kaeo, a refugee camp in Thailand. Puma was asleep on his father's back when the morning sun warmed his face and the cold brisk air welcomed him back to reality. He yawned, then opened his eyes to explore his new surroundings. Crows hovered in circles above the campground. The camp was an open dirt field with a run-down wooden shack in the front and fifty white tents, lined up in rows, behind it.

As Puma's family approached, an older man came out of the shack. He wore a white T-shirt with a red cross imprinted on it. A short conversation followed, and he escorted them to a nearby tent. Puma jumped down from his father's back and stood there, in the entrance of the tent, investigating his new home. There were smoke stains on the off-white walls. It took Puma 15 footsteps from the entrance to reach the back of the tent. He settled in the middle of the tent, where his pregnant mother unloaded supplies off her back. She gathered rice and dried salted fish to make porridge.

4

"Go fetch some wood from the forest," she said to Puma.

He hesitated. The sun was setting, turning the sky dark blue and brownish orange. The breeze clashed against the tent walls, making a soft thunderous sound. Puma stood there, momentarily paralyzed. His heart pounded; his eyes widened. He looked at his mom and said, "I don't want to go."

"What are you scared of? Go with your dad. Hurry." But he refused.

Even when his father lifted him into his arms, Puma suddenly kicked his dangling feet and broke free from his father's embrace. He ran outside to where his mother had gathered rocks and was placing them in a small circle to set up the fire. When Puma's father returned, breathing heavily, he dropped the sticks and branches in front of the pit and said, "A young woman with long black hair was roaming around in the dark. I called out to her, but she didn't answer."

Puma's mother paused and locked eyes with her husband. A chill came over her body, and her face tightened. The wooden spoon in her hand dropped to the ground. She picked up the spoon, poured water to rinse it, and said, "I saw her earlier when I went to draw water." The smoke from the fire hit her face and diverted her attention back to cooking.

Weary and consumed by hunger, Puma sat in front of the fire, under the spell of the blue, yellow, and reddish-orange flames beneath the pot. He gawked at the hot porridge bubbling inside the pot. His mother handed him a steaming bowl of porridge with dried fish on top. Puma's mouth watered. His little hands reached out to receive the meal. The smell of salty dried fish reminded him of home. He tore a piece of fish, dipped the aluminum spoon, inhaled and blew on the porridge. Shoving the spoon into his mouth, he chewed slowly, allowing the salty flavors to moisten every part of his mouth. He repeated that sequence till the last bite.

That night, nestled between his mom and dad, Puma slept on a full stomach. Suddenly his stomach roared and rumbled. He placed his right hand on his belly and rubbed it in a circular motion. Lying in silence in pain, he couldn't comfort his bloated belly. As his stomach continued to rumble, he focused on the apex of the tent. Puma's mother lay on her side next to him. He could feel the warmth of her bulging belly next to his elbow. Afraid to wake everyone, he lay there staring and listening to the moving walls of the tent. The longer he stared, the bigger and closer the walls seemed to get.

As he watched the walls, he heard noises coming from outside: sounds of whistling winds and crickets chirping. While listening to the sounds and watching the walls, a dark shadowy figure appeared. It walked slowly past. Tingling sensations arose throughout Puma's body. The hairs on his arms stood up. He closed his eyes. When he opened them again, the shadowy figure had gotten bigger. In slow motion the figure penetrated the wall of the tent, revealing its head. Long black hair covered its face and eyes, yet exposed its nose and lips. It leaned forward with half its body inside the tent. It stood above Puma, staring into his eyes. Puma felt the figure's hair skim across his face. His heart sped up, and he felt a cold nudge on his elbow. When he turned to look, he locked eyes with a pale woman.

"Wake up!" his father shouted. "You were screaming."

Tears trickled down Puma's face. His body trembled. "I want to go home," he cried.

Puma's father placed his hand on Puma's head and massaged it. "Tomorrow. I will ask the elders to hold a ritual ceremony to chase evil spirits away."

"I'm scared she will come back."

"I won't let anyone hurt you," his father said calmly.

Puma looked at his father, leaned his head on his chest, and wrapped his arm around him. His father pulled the blanket up to Puma's neck. Puma's heartbeat slowed, his breathing softened. Nestled against his father, Puma gently closed his eyes.

New
Kamsan Suon

New time for strife
New ways to survive
New lingering pain
New life

New living condition
New living arrangement
New broken down homes, shanties

New lost eyes
New tearful faces
New saddened looks
New mindless neighbors

New poor foods
New rats and lizards
New crickets and larvas
New starving days

New body shapes
New body weights
New breathing skeletons

New black pajama shirts
New black pajama pants
New black collectives

New slanted eyebrows
New blinkless eyes
New straight line lips

New masters in black
New masters with red and white checkered scarves on their necks and waists
New masters blasting AK-47s

New generation of turmoil!

Fish Out of Water
Hieu "Rocky" Nguyen

My father was a military officer for the South Vietnamese army, and was executed when I was only a couple of months old. At the time of my father's assassination, my family was forced into the Communist reeducation camp Xa Bang, where I was born and raised.

I spent nine years in that reeducation camp, where I witnessed violence, starvation, and murder. I would often see my mother grieving at night, and I would wake up in the dark and ask her what was wrong. She would tell me to go back to sleep. My mom was forced to work in the rubber jungle, where she had to scrub trees to harvest the rubber. Life in the camp was difficult, and food was hard to find. Every week my mom would go to the cooperative post where she was given two scoops of rice and one scoop of salt that would have to last us a whole week.

I would eat one day, then starve for the next two to three days. I remember when I was five years old, my brother and I found some manioc roots and were very happy. But on the way home, we were brutally beaten and robbed. They used a stick and cracked my head open. My mom did not have any money for my medical treatment, so she put tobacco on my wound to stop the bleeding. Around the same time, my mother gave away my oldest sister and brother because she was having difficulty raising five children on her own. When I was six, I often would go out and help my mom harvest rubber in the jungle. That was the first time I witnessed someone who had been robbed and murdered. His body was tied up on a rubber tree. I was so scared I froze. After that incident, my mom stopped having me help her in the jungle. Growing up in the camp, I felt scared most of the time. I did not get to go to school, and the only way I could learn was from my older sisters. They would teach me how to read and write.

When I was nine years old, my grandma came and took us out of the camp. We went to live with her in Bien Hoa. That was the first time I got to go to a real school. Due to my lack of education, I was slow at learning.

As I recall, one of my teachers was named Ho. He was a former Communist soldier and had lost his right leg in the war. Every time he showed up to the class drunk, he would verbally and physically abuse me. I recall him telling me that my father was a traitor and my family did not deserve anything, not even our lives. He hit me with a stick and constantly said that I was stupid just like my father for having supported the United States in the war. I was hurt and embarrassed in front of the whole class. I felt ashamed, helpless, and unworthy. Many times, I would walk home in tears, filled with bottled-up resentment. I thought about my father and wished that he were still alive to protect me. This abuse scarred me for life, and I would often hide in the dark so others would not see me.

My family was very poor. The place where I lived was about ten minutes away from the US military base Long Binh. I would go there with other kids in the village to look for gunpowder that we could sell. That was when I saw people get blown up by landmines.

On New Year's Eve of 1991, at the age of 11, I witnessed my neighbor, who was twenty years old, hanging around with my cousins and gambling. The Communist soldiers chased him and shot at him, and he was killed. I was terrified and scared. The event was so traumatizing that I did not want to leave my house during the whole week of that New Year.

During my school years, I was constantly teased by other kids. They made fun of me due to my mom selling bread and potatoes on the street. I did not understand why these kids were so mean to me, especially when I did not do anything wrong to them. I could not change my mom or where I came from. It hurt me to be rejected, and I became ashamed of who I was. That was when I told myself that I needed to do whatever it took to survive. I started to skip school and steal food from the markets. I wanted to have enough food to eat like other families.

When I was 14, the Humanitarian Operation interviewed my family and we were granted asylum due to my father's military service. My family arrived in Milpitas, California. There were a total of six of us, and we were living in a two-bedroom apartment on Calaveras Boulevard where we didn't have any furniture and there was only one mattress, so my older brother and I had to sleep on the floor. My mother would often walk around the neighborhood to look for trash bags filled with discarded clothes. She always asked me to go with her, but I didn't want to and would always say no. But I always ended up going with her because she did not speak English and I was worried that she might get lost. This situation reminded me of begging for food in the reeducation camp when we didn't have anything to eat, and how shameful it had been for me. I felt really powerless and unworthy. We lived in that apartment for over a year before we moved to Bixby Drive.

During my freshman year, I was enrolled at Milpitas High School. I was placed in ESL (English as a second language) classes. I often got teased and made fun of by other students because of the way I looked and talked. They called me many different names: "ching chong," "chino," "Chink." I remember during a PE class, while we were playing horseshoes, a student who was bigger than me took the horseshoe away from me and pushed me out of my spot. I was upset and angry, but I did not know how to express myself because my English was limited. I was afraid to fight him because he was bigger than me, so I told myself that I would seek revenge on him later. During this time, I was also working at McDonald's. I was there for about five months. I started off as a cook and was later promoted to cashier because my manager wanted to help me practice my English. I was happy and excited until one evening, when an abusive customer came in. He ordered a number 1 meal that included a Big Mac, large fries, and a drink. The total was $3.24, and he gave me $3.25. I refunded his one cent, and he took that penny and threw it in the trash can. He went on with his meal, and when he finished his drink he asked for a refill, so I granted his request. As he was walking out, he said that I didn't fucking speak English and who the fuck was allowing me to do this job. He said I needed to go back to wherever the fuck I came from. I felt angry and humiliated when I heard his comments, and I jumped over the counter and tried to assault him but was stopped by my manager. After that incident, I quit my job because I was embarrassed and afraid that my co-workers would make fun of me.

At about the same time, my home life was dysfunctional. My family barely communicated with each other. My mother worked as a maid and babysitter. She did not know how to cope with the pain and grief from her experiences living in the reeducation camp, witnessing my father's execution, and enduring persecution. Emotionally, she was detached from us. I did not know at the time that my mother was also dealing with hemorrhoids and cancerous tumors in her stomach.

She was diagnosed with what is now known as PTSD. She had difficulty sleeping and took medications constantly for both her stomach and for sleep. My brother, on the other hand, unable to cope with the stress, became an alcoholic. Every day he came home very late after work and was intoxicated. He was diagnosed with seizures that were a result of the head injuries he had suffered at the camp. He too had to take medication daily for his condition. As for my three sisters, one moved out of the state, and the others often stayed at their boyfriend's houses. At my home, we never ate together as a family. When I came home from school, the house would be empty. Often I felt sad and lonely. To cope, I began to stay after school and hang out with friends. That was the only time I felt I belonged.

During my first school year in America, I did not do well. I was told that I needed to take summer classes to improve my grades. In the summer of 1996, a couple of friends and I were hanging around at the bus stop after school. While waiting, we decided that we wanted to take the bench that was filled with students who had gotten there before us. So we came over and demanded that the students give us their seats. When they said no, we assaulted them. As a result, I was arrested and was sent to juvenile hall for a month. When I got out, I was placed on probation and house arrest. When I came back for my sophomore year, I noticed that my friends respected me more because of this incident. On the outside, I acted like I was a tough guy. But deep inside, I was a hurt little boy.

On October 6, 1996, my oldest sister passed away unexpectedly from cancer. It hit me really hard, and I felt like I had lost half of myself. My house became a stressful and anxious place for me. It hurt me so bad that I told myself I did not want to live like this anymore. So I ran away from home. I started to hang out with gang members, and I found validation and acceptance from a gang called VL (Vietnamese Lunatic). The gang offered me a place where I could act out without judgment. At the age of 16, I began cutting classes so I could hang out with the gang. I felt like I belonged with my friends because they accepted me for who I was. They did not care where I came from or if I knew how to speak English. I started stealing people's property, carrying weapons, bullying my peers, and fighting rival gang members. I was caught up in the vicious cycle of addiction to a gang and criminal lifestyle, and I was willing to commit crimes and harm innocent people. This led me to commit my life crime on July 20, 2000.

Video Vault Unlocked
Hung T. Ly

|| Unreleased: clips from a mental video archive. This is the UNLOCK.||
It begins in the early '90s.

"Over there!" yells the driver
in a Nissan coupe, pointing up in my direction.
An order prompts the front seat passenger to pull out a handgun.

Pop　　　　the glass-cracking sound　　　　the black tires screeching

It's the very first time Asian gangsters try to kill me.
Bad aim, coupled with a quick-flight reaction, and the round misses me.
A single bullet cracks the bedroom window. Discharged from a nine-millimeter.
The powerful impact of a potential life-ender.
Learned first-hand what "drive-by" meant
from the incident
The assailants—enemies of my big brother—
return several months later.
Gunfire riddles the walls of two bedrooms. But how can this be? No one hears the
shots. *Suppressed with silencers*—theory.
Avoided another attempt on my life. The thought of not waking up from a night's
rest—scary.
The camera's on sleep mode, identities remain a mystery.
A callous act preserved in anonymous history.
Do the gunners regret what they did?
Attempting to steal the future of an innocent kid.

In '93 I was only nine.

For over two decades I wished for a chance to return the bullets. I didn't want them, they weren't mine.

Three years later, a twelve-year-old delinquent.

Acceptance and reputation is what's relevant.

Pocket knives and fist fights, to drinking and smoking. Characteristics of a felon.

I soak up the lyrics of 2Pac's "Shorty Wanna Be a Thug." It's '96 going on '97.

Big brother, hauled off to prison.

Lack of positive role models—vulnerable position.

Lock myself in the room—wall of separation.

Bottle everything up—no conversations.

Graduate to junior high. New faces and different crowds. Clique up with dysfunctional

teens, and rejects too.

Introduced to a culture of mean mugs, gang signs, or "where you from?" Instead

of civil smiles, fist dabs, or "how are you?"

Struggling with class assignments, I don't have a clue.

No respect for authorities, "don't tell me what to do."

"Ah-ma" advises me to stay in school, but I won't listen.

Waiting for the perfect time, I dash across the intersection.

Missed the teacher's lesson.

End up in Saturday School—detention.

In the early 2000s, vengeful feelings flood my unstable teenage mind.

Anger, hate, fear, hypervigilance. Poisonous side effects from

atrocious acts of mankind.

Lack of control and communication skills, with alcohol abuse.

Ingredients of this ticking time bomb. Running on a short fuse.

Perception operating with clouded lenses. Distorted panorama.

User error, not a faulty camera.

Feel the need to protect myself, I find my own nine-millimeter.

It's a matter of time, before I pull the trigger.

Sick of being the victim,

so I switch positions, from flight to fight. And recklessly create my own victims.

"No one can ever hurt me again," I'm untouchable.

Saw the fear in others' eyes, I felt incredible.

At nine years plus ten, like my perpetrators, I was a gang member.

My right to freedom rescinded, when the detective said, "We're going to lock you up forever!"

Eventually,

the resentment caused by these episodes

evaporated. But like a stain,

difficult to erase, the memory remains.

||Archive: this is the END. One vault closes, another begins.||

Author's Note: Please understand that I am in no way making excuses for or glorifying my actions, seeking pity, or blaming others for how my life turned out. Today, I can honestly accept full responsibility for making the choice to assume the role of a criminal, which ultimately caused me to be locked away for public safety. This new way of living has allowed me to become more open-minded, empathetic, and optimistic.

In order to remain on the path of recovery and to become a prosocial member of the human race, my lens undergoes daily maintenance. It's my intention to capture a clearer and brighter unseen future.

This piece is dedicated to all crime victims who have lost their lives or suffered physical and mental pain from the misdeeds of others—as well as the victimizers who have broken the cycle of violence and are actively making amends to society for their actions.

"Please give me the strength and courage to continue in this process of growth and healing."

— *Si Dang, "Resentment & Forgiveness"*

MEMORY

**Art by
Havannah Tran**

My Name
Kamsan Suon

My name is this feeling
He cannot feel it

This boy is just too weak
He cannot speak it

My name has only two sounds
Yet, you don't have any strength to utter one

How can you
With that Lost Look in your Eyes
See Ourselves in Paradise?

My His-Story:
Growing Up A Half Breed in the USA
John V. Apollo

I am from my father, whom I never met, who is from a village on the island of Kauai, surf-beach-sea-shells, hales grass homes, and lomi-lomi salmon. I'm from Hawai'i when Hawai'i was a so-called territory of the USA, and today is a so-called state. I'm from a place where Anglo multinational corporations now have both big hotels and resorts, etcetera, etcetera, but from where, I do know as fact, true Kanakas do not recognize Hawai'i as a state, nor did they recognize it as a territory before it became a state! So be it. (Smile)

What I know about my mother's life? To be truthful, what I know about my mother's life is very little, except that she was very close to her famiglia and that she truly loved me!

I'm from my mother, who moved from Southern Italia and came to Ellis Island at 15 years of age, by her older husband, whom she later divorced. I'm from "the Big Apple," watching a WASP woman in a tenement window yelling at my 16-year-old half sister pushing a baby carriage, "Guinea, get off the sidewalk, you don't belong around here, go back to where you came from!" I'm from my aunt's house across the Hudson River to New Jersey, where my mother used to send me, every summer from 9 to 13 years of age. One day my mother had come to visit her sister, when an Anglo neighbor next door, who had been sweeping her porch, saw my mother and "yelled" at her to get off the sidewalk and walk in the gutter. She threatened her with the "straw broom" she had in her hand!

I'm from my stepdad, who was a Puerto Ricano nationalist, who believed that Puerto Rico should be an independent island nation! I'm from Spanish Harlem, where I lived from 4 to 13 years of age. I'm from mainly Black and Puerto

21

Ricano elementary and junior high schools, with some Southern Italianos and Jewish students in Harlem. And I say right on to that! I'm from homemade bacalao, rice and beans, chicken, and plátanos. I'm from a place where there is always music in the streets with a beat, congas, bongos, drums, pachanga, mambo, rumba, and salsa. I'm from a place where boys, girls, men, and women dress in bright colors—red, orange, purple, and yellow! I'm from stickball and hockey in the streets. I'm from fighting for survival whenever I went out of the barrio, anywhere else in the city! I'm from the smells of cooking, baking, frying, roasting fish, chicken, and pork. I'm from sweet and flaky pastries. I'm from fast walkers. I'm from summertime watermelons, mushmelons, honeydews, and cantaloupes. Viva Boricua Libre!

I'm from coming to the mainland from Hawai'i when I was three. It was winter, and I had never seen snow before. I'm from being so small and falling straight down into snow so deep I could have drowned in it. I'm from a cold winter day, a few years later, freezing cold, talking to some girls, when a couple of members of a Jewish gang snuck up behind me and set my big heavy blue winter coat on fire with some wooden matches! It's a good thing that it was wintertime with snow all over, and I was quick in taking off the coat, or it could have gone very bad for me, as I could have gotten burned or worse! Ice-cold! Yes, too chilly to say the least!

I'm from "Lil Italia" in Brooklyn, where I lived from 13 to 15½ years of age. I'm from light and soft silks, flowers, perfume, cologne. I'm from people who wear black, blue, white, and tan. I'm from soft, instrumental music, opera. I'm from slow walkers. I'm from pizza shops and hero sandwiches.

I'm from my mother's Siciliana/Napoletana/Toscana style Italiana meals, her Siciliana-styled spaghetti made with olive oil, garlic, and butter! I'm from chicken cacciatore and spumoni ice cream with lots of pistachios.

I'm from my mother, who told me she always wanted me to grow up to be one of three things—a lawyer, a policeman, or a priest. Not a gangster. I'm from a place with bad influences and criminal organizations, and I had been in the youth house[1] for gang fighting. I'm from a street social worker, one other good influence in my life, who worked with street gang members to be my sponsor

---

1 Youth House: Juvenile Detention System in New York

and assist me in the right direction! He was truly an important male influence in my life since my mother and stepdad had separated when I was 13 years of age. This social worker must have been in his thirties, and he did not drink or smoke, use drugs, or curse. He was into weight training and bodybuilding and eating natural, healthy foods. Right on. So be it. He introduced me to the Police Athletic League, exercising, and martial arts, American-style! Haha! The street social worker influenced me, later on in my life, to get into weight training, gym exercises, and the original Asian martial arts!

I'm from racist so-called borders. I'm from where racism is alive and well if you are not a WASP but are a person of color of the Third World or of the Fourth World tribal lands! So be it. I'm from negative immigration experiences, specially if you were coming from Sicily, Napoli, or Calabria! It was all very racist! Just like how they treat Asians/Pacific Islanders/Caribbean Islanders, as well as Central and South American immigrants right here on the so-called border between the USA and Mexico. I'm from being a half breed, a paesano Southern Italiano, but my other half... I'm from being identified as a hoodlum and a gangster by police, judges, and district attorneys. I'm from fighting Anglo gangs of the Germans and the Irish. I'm from playing handball, going to Coney Island and the beach, etcetera, etcetera. Right on.

I'm from my mother's side, where people would always say, women and children should be seen and not heard by the male cousins, uncles, and brothers-in-law. I'm from parades and marches, for Saint Anthony, for Saint Joseph, in Spanish Harlem. I'm from special events! And celebrations! I'm from block parties where everyone in the neighborhood cooked and baked and brought out tables, chairs, and benches where people could sit and eat! Both sides of the street were blocked off! Right on. I'm from Lil Italia, where instead of a block party, the paesanos/paesanas would rent out a park, and bring all the food dishes and desserts and drinks to the park, and it was policed by the Southern Italian gangs from the neighborhoods! Right on.

I'm from the Museum of Natural History in The City, where a gang of German kids pushed me down the stairs when I was seven. I'm from groups of Southern Italiano and Puerto Ricano kids visiting Central Park and the lake and the zoo, getting jumped or chased out of the park by all the Anglo/German/

Irish, Jewish, and Polish gangs that were all over Central Park. I'm from joining other Southern Italiano and Puerto Ricano kids to protect ourselves from the majority of the racist, fascist, and yes, sexist street gangs that were all over the city. I'm from Lil Italia, where the Italiano gangs were well respected and had a reputation for being good street fighters! I'm from being bullied by kids four years older than me because I was a half breed.

I'm from Flatbush, Brooklyn, a mixed Italiano and Jewish neighborhood, where we moved when I was 15½ years of age after getting into trouble time and again for gang fighting, etcetera, etcetera, and I was getting a bad reputation with the police and going to the youth house[2]! I'm from a junior high in the Flatbush school district that, due to it being in an Anglo-Irish neighborhood, was called "the Flatlands," which was an all-Irish neighborhood. I'm from that day, in all truth, the very first time in my life, all 15½ years of my life, that I saw blonde and red-haired blue-eyed girls. As well as the boys, all the Celtics/ Scots and Anglos! There were a few other students at the school who were Southern Italianos or Jewish, but I was the only half breed in the high school! I'm from where that was both bad and good for me. Bad because I was a half-breed "Guinea" and "spic" to the boys, who were all in a tough Irish gang! And good because I was the only real Latino at the school, and good due to how I represented myself, in both personality and the way that I dressed, and my reputation as a fighter. I'm from being very popular with the girls at the school!

I'm from my mother always telling me to have compassion and mercy towards all peoples, no matter who they are. I'm from my uncles, who always told me to respect your elders and look after the young ones. I'm from my sisters, who always told me to respect girls and women and treat them as your equals! So be it. Out of my five half sisters, two of them were all-girls' gang leaders and two were street fighters! I'm from my half bro, who always told me, whenever I got locked up in the youth house[3], etcetera, that if anyone wanted to bully or jump me, to always take out the leader or the biggest or toughest of them all! I'm from my stepdad, who would always tell me, as young as I was at that time, not to get a girl pregnant, and that if I ever did, to be a man and take the responsibility, as a dad, to provide for them! So be it.
I'm from not knowing anything about Hawai'i until I was 18½ years old, when my mother and I had a serious sit-down about who my actual biological dad

---

2 Ibid
3 Ibid

was, who I had never known, as I'd had a foster dad and then my stepdad who'd raised me.

As to my Kanaka family? I never knew my grandmother or my granddad on my biological father's side! I do know that I would have relatives from my grandmother's side, as she was full-blood Kanaka!

And one day, I pray that I will be able to go back to try and locate my grandmother's side! So be it. (Smile)

My His-Story Where I'm From
I'm from my Southern Italiana mother
my dad, my Kanaka/Boricua biological dad

Closing my eyes, here is what I imagine—
my father growing up,
and as a lil boy
he loved
the surf/sea/swimming/fishing/coconuts
and natural original "Luau" of fish/seafood/birds!
And Poi!

Smile right on, right on, right on.
I picture my Kanaka family
thinking
(Smile)

Where I'm From,
I'm From THE UNIVERSE!!
(So be it)

American Dream
Remus James Langi

God knows they tried…
To raise me up the right way
Sacrificed, journeyed miles away
Just to give me better days
Left their homeland, all they knew
To pursue a dream come true
Something they wanted for me
Something they call…
The American Dream

Suffering lonesome long days
But shorter than my sleepless nights
I wake up searching for Momma
Searching for Daddy, both M.I.A.
Cooked instant Top Ramen
Microwaved bread, butter and sugar
Struggling to make ends meet
I've never seen so much praying

Praying to a god we've never seen
Praying to a god that they believed
Will deliver us from this nightmare
And realize our American Dream

Were we better off?
We've suffered so many losses
Cried homesick saltless tears

Missing our home, pacific ocean
Motion denied, lawyer's fee too high
Courtroom silenced as Momma cries
Crying helplessly for her child
She warned countless times

Praying to a god I've never seen
Praying to a god I now believe...
Will deliver me from this nightmare
And realize her American Dream

Running
Vu Bui

It was my first day of school in America.

I soon found myself in the front office of Morningside Elementary. After having traced the disappearance of my parents through a series of glass windows, I sat there in anticipation, waiting for further instructions.

Waiting, but more than that, surveilling. The need to decode the office technician's message. Her tone of voice. Her body language. Yup. Just another typical day at the office for a nine-year-old Vietnamese refugee.

The human traffic surrounded me, threatening to smother me, as my eyes kept watch. Then the door to my left, directly opposite the entrance, swung open. An unexpected sound—or voice, rather—punctured through the claustrophobic confine of antiseptic and flower perfume.

"Hi! Are you Vû?" Taken aback by hearing my name properly inflected, I instinctively turned and nodded at the stranger, who I figured to be about my age. Without other corroborating evidence, I was totally convinced that she was of Vietnamese descent. And, without further delay, the never-ending Tour of Confusion continued.

"I am Vi. Come on. Follow me!" Seized without a warrant, I held on in confused compliance. We quickly moved through the push door, then made a right turn, before launching down the winding, open corridor leading to my assigned classroom.

A customary handoff, and she was gone. Vi was my schoolmate. Morningside

Elementary, however, was quite expansive in size, and that encounter turned out to be the only interaction we had.

I wasn't overly concerned about the sudden departure of the friendly stranger, though, due to another pleasant surprise.

"Hello, Vu. Welcome to our classroom. My name is Ms. Apples and…" I didn't hear a thing beyond that because my mind was unhinged from uncontained excitement.

"Apple! Apple! Apple!" One of the few English words I knew.

Things were really looking up, I thought to myself. Maybe Mom and Pop were right. Maybe this America thing might be good for me after all.

I read somewhere that a child's mind is in a state of perpetual denial, due to an overwhelming need to believe that the world is safe. And that was where I found myself, grasping onto whatever I could for security.

Unfortunately, the Southern California school district, at least during the early '90s, wasn't equipped to meet the learning needs of culturally displaced children like myself. I didn't yet know that Morningside Elementary—and the American public school system as a whole—would be my first prison, and the criminal street gang, my first addiction.

To be fair, my parents went above and beyond their parental calls of duty, considering the burdens they carried each day of their lives. My father was 47, and my mother 41 when we left the old country in November 1993. Unification of Vietnam under communism, on April 30, 1975, was as hellish as it could get for many who were militarily connected to the South. For his role as an army officer during the conflict, my father was deemed "unlearned" by the new government and was consequently sent away for reeducation in various prison camps. He was promised a routine 12-day debrief, which abruptly became an indeterminate sentence, which then became a seven-year incarceration. State deception in place of due process.

My mother was then 23, with the weight of her family's welfare (my father plus three older siblings) now bearing down on simple life decisions. Then came the post-camp years prior to our transpacific flight. This is not an attempt to recount my parents' stories, the magnitude of which can only be framed within a larger context. I write as their son in exile, in desperate search of footholds to support me across a dark, uncertain reality.

No. The point here is that they were—and are—the best parents I could have ever hoped for. The details of my younger days are unaging. I recall Sunday school at the local Vietnamese Buddhist temples, private English and math tutoring sessions, and my two failed attempts at mastering kung fu via Tae Kwon Do and Vovinam. Triple up the enrollment plus monthly fees to include my siblings, and these activities amounted to a hefty investment... Nevertheless, what I needed at the time, more than anything else, was a parent-child relationship—a tangible sense of being valued and loved at home. In the absence of such, everything appeared unreal, like a movie. I remained at a standstill, totally unrelated to all that was alive and moving around me.

And it never occurred to me to ask for help.

I promptly learned that Ms. Apples had poor stress management. She never did warm up to me using her as a sparring partner for English 101. Talk about hating where you are. I came to dread each school morning: the harsh language that tortured my tongue, the boisterous classmates who wouldn't shut up, the surprisingly long-lasting carsickness, and—to make matters a thousand times worse—the bland, dry, tasteless cafeteria food.

The following events unfolded in a blur.

I began faking illnesses to leave school for home, where hours of side-scrolling, mind-numbing button mashing awaited. Deception, avoidance, and isolation—three skills I honed at a very young age.

I would come to learn that what I had wasn't simply a language barrier, but a crisis of identity that might never be truly resolved. Although my family had been flown over on the US government dime, some considered my siblings and me "fresh off the boat." For our peers, this label served as a warrant for discrimination.

Some wounds in life cut deep into your soul. They change how you see and feel about yourself. The rejection I experienced from my peers in my early years damaged me more than I'd like to admit. And there was my younger sister. She was two years my junior, and so fate allowed us to share many experiences: the good, the bad, and—because of my own negligence—even the ugly. Often we walked, in hurried but defiant steps, through alleys of racial slurs and death threats.

We lived within an ethnic encapsulation of Little Saigon—Westminster. There was an irony to the fact that our denouncers were almost exclusively other Vietnamese, who were American born and whose families had immigrated years prior, and thus had had ample opportunities to get situated.

A good number of my peers would saunter across the school campus with an air of superiority, coming out of shiny SUVs, garbed in fancy sportswear and brand-name backpacks. The line was clearly drawn between the haves and have-nots, and these snobbish peers were quick to remind me what I didn't have.

A historian once noted that the only two races of people who have been fighting throughout their history are the Vietnamese and the Irish. There has been a lifelong tendency to romanticize, oftentimes to my own detriment, this fighting spirit. The idea is that you hate and hate, and carry that hate forward until it becomes a movement. A revolution may be ignited by the fire of love, but it is built one resentment at a time. I began to stack mine.

Lesson by lesson, the miseducation continued until six years, two cities, and five schools later, I, as a freshman, decided there was nothing of value at home or at school. I felt alone and excluded from the world and those around me.

Pressure can really bust a pipe. The occasional school fights and hours of button mashing and kung fu movies no longer sufficed as coping outlets. I grew weary of simply stacking my resentments and began looking for reasons to cash in. During the summer between my freshman and sophomore years, everything finally boiled over.

A local neighborhood bully turned gang member aggressively approached me. I combusted. Outsized, unarmed, and trapped along a narrow alleyway with a chain-link fence behind Weber Elementary, I managed to get the would-be assailant to back off through sheer madness. Eye contact struck, maintained, and the outgoing message made clear: touch me and one of us will not make it out alive.

Though I was victorious, something vital at the core of my being broke during the exchange. What vague sense of self I had was no longer an essential factor. Despite my natural inclination toward decency and kindness, I developed mistrust and disdain for all who disagreed with me, including my parents. I became shortsighted. Tomorrow became a myth; I lived solely for the moment, having ruled out all possible futures. I was willing to do anything, to sacrifice everything, even my own physical well-being, for momentary payoffs.

Aggression became my leverage to make the world work.

Damn it all to hell. If I am not worth remembering, I'll be sure I'm hard to forget. Not long after the alleyway exchange, I sought out and ran with a local Vietnamese street gang. While I could have done without the brutal, red-carpet thrashing, it did not stop my rapid tailspin into baseless violence and moral decay. I believed this was the price of acceptance and respectability.

According to Vietnamese tradition, there are four measures of a man: material wealth, beautiful women, heavy drinking, and unyielding masculinity. I was driven to set a new record.

But the bottomless pit of cravings, conditioned by emotional turmoil, cannot be filled with these things. They do not last. Buddhism's first law? Impermanence. Second law? Suffering. Both summed up by the truth that things by nature do not last. When they pass, pain and sorrow oftentimes follow.

On March 20, 2007, after three long years in an Orange County jail, at 22 years of age, I was convicted and condemned to a prison term of 35 years to life. The higher the climb, the harder the fall. Indeed, when the dust settled, I had to reconcile the nightmarish truth that my life no longer belonged to me.

I had lost everything, including a long-term relationship with a remarkable woman who loved me in ways I believed I would never be loved again. After the verdict was announced, my pride wouldn't allow her to see me in such a devastated state. So I did what I thought any respectable Vietnamese gentleman would have done to protect his ego: I sent her a Dear Jane letter.

If you're going nowhere, any road will get you there. As idiotic, pitiful, and lost as this expression sounds, it poetically defines my early years in state penitentiary, from April 2007 to January 2012. Two uneventful months at the Wasco reception center, then a transfer to Kern Valley State in Delano, a level 4 maximum-security institution. Clashes between Asians and Pacific Islanders ensued. As a 23-year-old first termer, my logic was simple: just do what the other Vietnamese do.

People plan, God dictates, as my mother says. In her maternal wisdom, my mother theorizes a "thick skull" to explain my lifelong stupidity. People like me, she concludes, will inevitably change, but only along with pain. Indeed, it would take another six years of losses and a thorough life beatdown before the scale tipped in favor of change.

January 23, 2012, Salinas Valley State Prison. In the aftermath of an early morning raid systematically targeting the Asian and Pacific Islander inmate population, I found myself thrown into a Security Housing Unit: a prison inside a prison, more popularly referred to as "the hole." My body struggled to balance itself in the absence of drugs and alcohol. I sat, alone now in a cell that was roughly 9 by 12 feet, underneath a catwalk no longer in use, suspended in a vacuum of self-hate and emotional confusion. The stainless steel glint from the combination sink-toilet four feet away was barely visible. It was minutes till midnight, and prison codes dictated that cell blocks on both wings be devoid of discernable sounds.

Silence, solitude, and sobriety—synergistic and potentially lethal for someone like me, a specialist in natural and manufactured chaos. Quietude had never been an option.

The sensation of dread was familiar. Unconsciously, I gasped for air while my body contracted in tension. The unfinished business of my childhood—fear, anger, guilt, and shame—came back to exact some form of settlement.

Lights on. Shields up. All systems ready. But to fight…or flee?

That was the defining moment. It marked the beginning of a time where the pace of events appeared to slow down for me. It wasn't just a blur anymore. I understand today that there are two ways to look at F.E.A.R.: either we "forget everything and run" or "face everything and rise." For the first time in my life, at 28 years of age, I opted for the latter. I chose to meet life where it was, to sit through and look at the underlying pain and anguish I had been carrying—and feeding. Getting up from that proverbial "blanket of depression," I decided to unstack the mountain-high resentments that were crushing me. In the wake of a hurricane, there is the work of reconstruction. I realized the rubble—problematic beliefs, values, and attitudes—had to be cleared out. But I was stuck on this question: What would be the new foundation onto which this new house of self would be built?

There's a runaway kid in me today who has to be nurtured and watched over, even at 35 years old—because in many ways, I have never stopped running since landing at John Wayne Airport in 1993. From motion sickness to motion addict, it will take ten years of sitting meditation before I learn to stop and ground myself in the present moment.

And, more importantly, to reverse direction.

A good friend taught me, "There are no bad people, only bad decisions." And to remember to always look for the person inside the behavior. Today, in February 2020, drug-free and law-abiding, I instinctually run towards meaning and healing, back in time. Through concrete walls, gun towers, and barbed wire fences, I retrace my steps through the winding, open corridors of Morningside Elementary. Passing by dear Ms. Apples, Vi, and the busy-looking office technician to finally find who I am looking for. I spot the boy and draw nearer. I ask permission to sit close. I ruffle his jet-black, Bruce Lee haircut and offer him a reassuring look. I tell him, in his native tongue, that he is right about America being a good thing. Because it is in this land that he will find his chosen method of moving through life: compassion.

Resentment & Forgiveness
Si Dang

Dear Father,

This is your youngest son, Si. It has been nearly thirty years since you left our family without saying goodbye. It's important for me to write you this letter to express how your actions and inactions have affected me. Please know that it's not easy for me to write this letter because of the love and respect I have for you. I hope this letter will lead us toward a path of forgiveness and healing from pain, sorrow, fear, shame, and disappointment.

It is not my intention to offend you with my words, nor is it my desire to bring up our family's past, but it's important for you to know how your actions have created a lot of sadness in my heart. This is not to blame you for any of my wrongdoings, because I am solely responsible for all of my actions and poor choices. Please find it in your heart to forgive me for being bold, blunt, and honest with you.

In 1987, when I was 11 years old, I witnessed your rage and violent behavior in a terrifying event that took place in our home. Please allow me to refresh your memory with the details of what happened on that night.

It was a beautiful and quiet evening. My mother had cooked a delicious meal for our family, as she did every night with the limited resources that we had. My siblings and I were starving and waiting for you to come home so that we could eat together. When you walked through the front door, I could smell the odor of alcohol on your breath and knew that you had come back from drinking with your so-called friends. Although the lingering smell of liquor fuming from your breath and clothes was strong, I was too blinded by my own hunger to notice how drunk you were. We gathered around the dinner table and sat down, anticipating a wholesome meal together. I was joyful, expecting to finally put some food in my empty stomach. Suddenly, you did something unexpected and unthinkable!

My concerned mother politely asked, "Are you okay? Why are you late for dinner?" Immediately, you stood up from your seat with a clenched fist and punched her square in the face. The blood from her nose squirted all over the food as she screamed in excruciating pain. She ran to the kitchen to grab a towel to stop the red flow of blood streaming from her nose as you belligerently screamed at her. As I turned around in my chair to look for my mother, I saw that the white towel pressed against her face was soaked and stained with blood and tears. I wasn't sure if her tears were the result of the pain and shame she felt from your action or from the impact of your strike. Either way, I knew my mother was in agony from your violent act. A mother's love and sense of protection quickly kicked in and, still holding the bloody towel to her face, she rushed her children into the bedroom to safeguard them from further harm. Just like a mother hen, she swiftly rushed her little chicks into the coop, wanting to protect them from being devoured by a hungry wolf.

Before being rushed into the bedroom, I saw you storm off toward the family's altar and smash the Goddess of Mercy statue against the floor. The white porcelain statue shattered into little pieces, which scattered around the fireplace. I was terrified and shocked. My body froze until my older sister Tuyet grabbed my arms and quickly guided me to the bedroom. As the door slammed shut behind us, I heard a thunderous argument between you and my mother echoing loudly through the thin plaster walls. My siblings and I trembled with fear as we balled together under a blanket, hoping that we could keep each other safe from you. We went to bed hungry and frightened by the chaotic event on that dark evening.

I tried to force myself to sleep that night, but it was impossible because I was worried about my mother's safety and well-being, and not knowing what had happened to her made me even more fearful. My inability to protect her from your brutality made me feel like a coward and an unworthy human being. I hated myself for not being able to stand up for my vulnerable mother, and you don't know how much I wanted to hurt you. As a result of the hurt, fear, and shame I felt in that moment, I made a promise to myself to protect and defend at all costs the people who were closest to me and those who were vulnerable. This promise I made to myself would later have dire consequences in my life.

The following morning, I saw you sitting silently near the fireplace with your chin gently resting on your palm as you stared blindly into the flames. I have always wondered what was going through your mind at that moment. From the outside, I saw a man who was filled with sorrow, pain, hurt, shame, and regret. I wanted to forgive you because I saw the deep sadness and guilt on your face, but I couldn't muster the courage to do so. Sadly, I held on to my burning resentment toward you, and the bitter hatred multiplied as I looked at my mother's bruised and battered face for what seemed like an eternity. The gruesome images of her bloody face were seared into my mind, and it fueled the burning anger in my heart, like a flaming iron rod. My resentment toward you was powerful enough to incinerate a human soul from existence. After that terrifying night, something inside me died—my sense of innocence had been stolen from me. The beauty of the world and the bright future I had once hoped for quickly vanished into thin air. In many ways, your act of violence reshaped the way I viewed people and my environment. After that incident, I didn't feel safe or protected anymore. Instead of seeing the world as a beautiful place to live, I saw it as a place filled with danger and chaos. The pain in my heart lingered as the years passed, and it wasn't until later that I realized the negative impact it had on me.

On March 31, 1989, when I was 13, you and three of our relatives were tragically killed in a car accident that left our family in so much grief and confusion. I can clearly remember that painful day as if it happened yesterday. That evening, I was outside looking up at the skies feeling conflicted about what I was seeing and how I was feeling. The skies were beautifully painted with purple, red, light orange, yellow, and a stroke of bluish gray. It was as if the Creator had dipped his colossal hand into a river of colors and then applied a swift stroke across the canvas of the sky. As majestic as the heavens looked, I had a strange intuition that something horrible was about to happen. Not wanting to think about it, I brushed off the feeling and strolled into the house. My siblings and I were sitting at the dinner table getting ready to eat when the phone rang, and after three rings, my oldest brother, Anh Hay, picked up the phone. He answered, "Hello! Who is this?" After a few seconds, Anh Hay said to the caller, "Slow down. What happened?" Almost instantly, my brother's tone of voice changed from calm to fearful, and his face turned white. I immediately knew something terrible had happened. Anh Hay handed the phone to my older sister, Chi Tuyet, took the car keys from the kitchen counter, and dashed out the door. After hanging up the phone, Chi Tuyet informed us that there had been a car accident that involved you, Mom, Suong, and other relatives. I was confused, lost, and in disarray. The next morning, my intuition became an apocalyptic reality that forever changed our lives. Our family grieved and mourned for you and our relatives in silence. I am truly sorry that I was unwilling to properly mourn your death because of the resentment I had toward you. I was a young kid in pain who was blinded by anger.

For many years, I refused to forgive you for the heartaches you caused our family. I blamed you for all the terrible things I had done to other people and for the crimes I had committed. I was an irresponsible person both in my thinking and in my behavior. When I was 15, I began hanging around with gang members and criminals. A year later, I decided to join a gang, which brought much shame and disgrace to our family. If you had been alive to see it, I think you would have been devastated by my behavior. But I didn't care about myself at the time, and I definitely wouldn't have cared how you felt. On the morning of March 7, 1996, I made the worst decision of my life when I murdered my victim and attempted to murder another. I was apprehended and then convicted of these heinous crimes and was sentenced to 35 years to life. I am remorseful about Andy's death and the attempted murder of Sen Dang and the pain and grief I've caused Andy Tran's and Sen Dang's family and friends.

Father, you would have assumed that receiving a life sentence and going to prison would somehow inspire me to change and become a better person, right? On the contrary, throughout my years of incarceration, I continued to live a pathetic and disgraceful lifestyle like I did when I was in society. I truly regret this because I harmed countless lives in so many ways.

On numerous occasions behind these prison walls, I wished you had been there to lend me guidance and support when the world seemed so dark, lonely, and hopeless. Although my resentment toward you burns like a flaming torch, my love for you has always been there. I wanted to make myself hate you for hurting our family, but the truth is that I needed your love and affection.

On August 18, 2012, I received a disciplinary infraction for possessing a cell phone. Three days after the incident, I was alone in my cell around midnight, twisting and turning on my bunk bed, unable to fall asleep. A thousand doubts and questions raced through my mind, keeping me awake, but it seemed like there were gigantic walls blocking me from the land of answers and truth. I was frustrated, doubting that I would find any answers, so I got off my bunk and began pacing back and forth in my cell. I didn't realize how dark and silent it was at that time of night, when others were sleeping, studying, or doing what I was doing, thinking and reflecting. I turned on the light, and I looked past my cell bars and saw the reflections of the light from my cell bouncing off the building windows. I felt confused, lonely, empty, and defeated. The same feelings I felt when you were suddenly killed in that horrific car accident. I fell to my knees and prayed to you, asking for guidance and wisdom to help me through my confusion. I was filled with guilt and shame, and I cried for hours, unable to stop the tears. It was like a stream of water flowing down from the mountains into the river. Although I didn't find the answers I was looking for that night, I discovered something even more important: the ability to let myself cry. I hadn't cried since I was 14 years old, when I was beaten up by three kids at school. At the time, I hadn't cried because of the pain and bruises on my body but because of the humiliation and embarrassment that I felt in my heart and soul. After that incident I vowed never to cry again, butI violated my oath that night, and I felt relief. And I made a new vow to stop living the criminal lifestyle, and it's a vow I am committed to.

I was on the path of healing and determined to search for answers to the lingering questions. I had a newfound desire to talk with my mother and siblings. Hours later, as I looked outside my cell bars, I could see the bright yellowish-orange sunlight rising above the horizon of the prison walls. It was time for me to get up, and I was excited to create a road map to explore our family's history, culture, and roots. I now knew where to go for help to find the answers I was seeking.

My mother and siblings shared many stories about your childhood that involved your alcoholic father and how his abusive behavior affected you. In addition, my mother spoke with teary eyes about the death of your mother when you were a teenager, which left you with a broken heart. Father, you held a lot of pain and sorrow inside of you, and the inability to share it with people turned it into a compressed atomic bomb waiting to explode. I recognized how your frustration and anger from losing someone you loved so dearly tormented you for decades. I empathize with your misery from being abused by your father, and it pains me to think about the overbearing struggles and sorrows that we experienced during our childhoods, because I strongly believe no child should have to suffer the way we did. I can only imagine the strength and courage that you must have possessed to be able to manage your agony and heartaches. I often wonder, Have I inherited your strength and courage? I wish I could say yes.

After we spoke about your childhood, we talked about the Vietnam War and your military service fighting against the North Vietnamese Communist Party. My mother told me about the harmful impact the war had on you. It was eye opening for me to get a glimpse of the horrific experiences you went through— witnessing the deaths of your best friends, cousins, relatives, neighbors, and civilians, and narrowly escaping death yourself. She expressed to me that after the war ended in April 1975, you returned home to your family as a different person. Although you were responsible and caring, you were also distant, disconnected, isolated, easily agitated, silent, and drowning in emotional pain that you probably couldn't understand. After the war ended, you were arrested by the vengeful Communist government and sent to a reeducation camp. The trauma of living in constant fear did not allow you the time and space to recover from your physical and emotional pain. No war is a good war, and those who have experienced the carnage of war continue to suffer the battle scars silently in their hearts and minds. Even though you were no longer fighting against combatants on the battlefield, the war caused you to fight an invisible enemy within yourself. I want to ask you to please be at peace and allow the pain to ease so that you and the people you love can heal with you. Father, please know that the courage you showed by serving in the military to defend a nation in turmoil makes you no less than a hero in my eyes.

Lastly, we spoke about your sacrifices and the difficult decision you made to flee Vietnam so that our family could have the opportunity to have a better life in the United States. I can only imagine the pain and sorrow of making

41

the decision to leave your father, brothers, sisters, friends, relatives, and homeland behind to take on the treacherous journey to an unknown future. I truly appreciate your ultimate sacrifice to provide our family with a chance to succeed in America. Although life has not been an easy journey, in many ways our family did succeed in attaining the American Dream. In addition, your six children have given you nine beautiful grandchildren. If you were alive today, I am certain that you would love them with all your heart and shower them with love and affection. I am also certain that they would love and appreciate your unconditional love for them.

Thank you for all the times you showed your love as a father and a husband, and please know that your courageous spirit will always live inside our hearts. I am so sorry for all the wrongs I have done and the pain and hurt I have caused you, our family, and many others. I humbly ask for your forgiveness, and I vow to become a better person every day as I continue to learn and grow. I am striving to be the best I can. Please give me the strength and courage to continue in this process of growth and healing.

Father, it is my duty as a son to humbly ask for forgiveness, and forgiving you is my responsibility to our family. Please, rest in peace. Our family loves and misses you very much. I will always love you, my dear father.

Your son,

Si Van Dang
July 21, 2017

From Growing Up to Growing Pains
Saiyez Ahmed

Migrating to the US at six years of age was an adventure for me. But at the same time, it was sad because I was leaving behind the place where I was born and the only home I knew. My grandma wanted us to leave the islands of Fiji because she wanted all of us to have more and better opportunities in life. I understand her position—Fiji is small, and there's not much going on there. It's a slow and peaceful life, and I know many people would love to have that lifestyle, but you need money to survive comfortably.

After moving from one relative to another for about two years, we finally settled down in Richmond, California. Back then I didn't know the reputation Richmond had. I enrolled in school, and it was the first time I was able to leave the house on my own. You can imagine how naive I was. I had no idea what fashion was, and my mom picked my clothes for me. We didn't have much money, so the best places to shop for everything were Kmart and Newberry's. That's where I got all my clothes and shoes. Kids at school were mean as hell, but what they didn't understand was that they were changing my perspective on things. I came into this country thinking everyone was the same and that we should help to pick up those who are less fortunate, but through being made fun of because of who I was and my lack of funds to be in tune with the fashion trends, I realized that money was important and everyone wasn't equal. Being an immigrant is not easy in the beginning, and I know a lot of immigrants who were treated badly or who experienced racism and bullying, just like me.

Those are not good experiences for anyone to have to deal with at a young age, and they change you for better or for worse. For me, it was for worse. I prioritized two things: don't be broke, and don't let anyone disrespect you. My goal was to get money and help my family. I did not want my mom to struggle or my two little siblings to go through the things I had experienced.

By the time I was 13, I had anger issues and got into so many fights that I started to enjoy them. I particularly disliked bullies, so I would challenge them at every opportunity. When I began getting arrested, I met people from different areas and got involved with drug dealing and gangs. By the time I was 23, I'd been rejected from CYA[4] and ended up in Pelican Bay SHU[5] for cutting another guy's throat. Prison and other places of incarceration did not change me for the better—they made me worse. I also never applied myself to becoming a better person.

Currently, I am serving a sentence of 25 years to life under the Three Strikes law. I was denied parole for five years due to my disciplinary record and the lack of emotional remorse for my victims. I never planned to go to the board[6], so I kept on getting into trouble throughout my years of incarceration—it's been 22 years now. But things happened that I would never have imagined. I lost my little brother in 2009 and my little sister in 2018. My mom is blind, and only my dad is there to help her now. I hate the way it makes me feel—that I'm letting them down every passing day by not being there for them.

My little siblings looked up to me, and we were very close. As long as I knew my little brother and sister were taking care of Mom, I didn't care what happened to me. I had left enough out there for everyone to be able to live decently well and to take care of my family.

For a long time, I thought money would make me happy. I never considered what I was putting my family through. I was selfish because I was only thinking about my own feelings. It felt good to be able to give money to my family whenever they needed it. But the security I thought I had established for them slowly faded away as the bills and medical concerns—as well as my own grief—piled up.

Living the way I was had effects on everyone. Choices I made did more than just lock me up—they also slowly broke my family apart. Every day I feel the guilt and helplessness. Not being able to do anything or to be there for my parents is like living in a constant nightmare I can't wake up from. In a blink, I went from being content with my sentence to becoming miserable as I sit here hoping I have a chance to spend some time with my parents before they pass.

---

4 CYA: California Youth Authority
5 SHU: Security Housing Unit, otherwise known as Solitary Confinement
6 Board: Board of Parole Hearings

It's not easy to live like this and when the board[7] denied me, I was mad at them for keeping me from my mom. But that's the wrong approach, because I am the one who made the choices that landed me in this position. I am able to see that now and to accept that I am the one who made the mistakes. I responded to things in life in the wrong ways, and I didn't recognize it until it was too late. The old me slowly eroded away like a landscape changed by a river.

As you read this, you can see that my family was my priority, but what I was doing to help them was not the right path. I know with each passing day, I put stress on my ailing parents, who want me to come home. I have to do my part to accomplish this, because in the end, it's on me. Every time I was raided, arrested, or sent to the hole[8] in prison, I would say it wasn't my fault. I always blamed the snitches who told on me. Now that I reflect on it, I can see I'm always there doing something to cause my problems. I can say I wish I did things a different way or I wish I knew this or that—but, really, there is no right way to do the wrong things.

I hope my story—brief as it is—makes readers aware that actions have consequences. Our choices in life have to be considered carefully because sometimes we can hurt the people we hold dearest.

---

7 Ibid
8 Hole: Nickname for SHU

White World
Kamsan Suon

"It's snowing! It's snowing!" yelled Tom. I looked at him. He was a white American boy with blond hair and blue eyes. He sat a few rows to my right. Everyone in my first-grade class turned their heads and bodies the moment Tom yelled and looked at the windows behind me. What did he mean by "snowing"? What were they looking at? Although some of my classmates had accepted my different Cambodian features, I felt like an outcast. My tight and slanted eyes with dark skin looked strange in the new world. So what if my strangeness did not excite some of my American peers? I didn't let my strangeness keep me from learning. And I became best friends with Scott Parker. But he was not in class that day. I was sitting in the middle of the room and turned my head and body to look in the same direction as my classmates. I had begun learning the English language three months before.

Our teacher was Mrs. Brady, a nice white American in her mid-thirties. I trusted her. Tom had interrupted her morning math lesson. After a brief pause she told us we could go to the windows and look at the snow fall. Chair legs scraped on the tile white floor as everyone except me hurried to the windows. I stayed quiet and observed. I only knew the cold was outside.

Before my family of eight—including my parents—immigrated to America, I didn't know the cold existed. And when we relocated to Oklahoma City, Oklahoma, in 1981, it was August. One morning some months later, I went outside and discovered a strangeness in the air. I couldn't resist this new phenomenon. I wanted to explore it. I walked across the street to the park. I was wearing a T-shirt, pants, and rubber sandals. My body began to shiver. I found myself wrapping my arms around my chest. Then my toes, fingers, and ears became numb. But I didn't care about any of that. I thought it was funny when my teeth started clicking. I was amazed at how steam came out of my mouth. I pressed two fingers on my lips like my Dad did when he smoked cigarettes.

My mom yelled at me when I came inside our apartment about an hour later. "Don't go outside again." I asked her about the things I felt. She said that we now live in a cold country and it is the cold months, and everyone feels the same when they are in the cold. I didn't have a coat to wear until a week later.

Many Southeast Asian refugees wore used clothing. The good white Christian church folks had given us this clothing. I was grateful and happy to have a coat. It was a dull navy blue with a hood and a small yellow zigzag stripe across the chest. I wore it everywhere I went.

I envied my classmates who wore new clothing. They wore bright beanies that wrapped snugly around their heads. Others wore cotton gloves. I knew my family was poor, and I felt lucky to have my coat.

While I watched my classmates, I felt like it was my first day at school. I wanted to be part of the group. I left my seat and went to stand behind them near Becky. She was a white American girl with freckles on her face. She had auburn hair, and her smile made me feel comfortable. Becky was nice to me, but I was a shy boy. They were looking out the windows above the wood bookshelves. I saw nothing except for the grey clouds.

"Do you see the snow?" Becky asked. "What is snow?" I replied. "It's falling from the sky," she answered. I looked out the windows. I knew why I wasn't able to see it. Snow was white and blended in with the grey sky. It was drifting down slowly. I smiled. "When lots of snow falls, everything turns white," Becky said, smiling. I believed her but was concerned how that could be true. I couldn't see that image.

"We all can go outside to watch the snow fall," Mrs. Brady said. "Yeah!" some shouted. I stood there. My classmates put on their warm clothing and walked out of the classroom. "Kamsan," my teacher said at the door. "Come, let's go outside." My fear subsided with her smile. I grabbed my coat off the chair and put it on. I walked out with her by her side into the short hallway. The grey steel door that led out onto the playground was getting closer.

Mrs. Brady opened the door into a new world. "Chomm!" I said softly, which in Khmer meant "whoa/wow." I stood still in the doorway. A world was transforming right before my eyes. Trees and bushes began turning white. The soccer field had turned into a sheet with some small dark spots still on its surface. The benches, monkey bars, and roofs of homes nearby seemed so new.

Everyone and everything was covered in white. I walked out onto the black asphalt that was already changing into black and white dots. White snowflakes drifted continuously down around me, onto my head and shoulders. There was no way to escape the invasion of whiteness, not even in the space between me and the air. I thought it was fun when my classmates spun around with outstretched arms to each side. I reached out my arms to each side with palms up. I smiled as cold snowflakes gathered lightly on my tiny hands.

"In here, we tend to see each other as the enemy, without truly recognizing that we are not the ones who have placed the chains around our necks. But I can't fault us for our complacency. Maybe our eyes haven't fully opened yet."

— *Billy Gumabon, Open Eyes*

Art by
Gary Taylor

WITHIN
PRISON

Open Eyes
Billy Gumabon

I've been locked up for eight years now and I've been transferred a few times, but this time felt like a different experience. Maybe my eyes are a little more open these days. This time, I really felt like a piece of property being moved, like chattel. The process of being stripped naked, searched, chained from my ankles to my wrist, put into an orange jumpsuit, then loaded onto a bus highly secured by men with shotguns and AR-15s... I couldn't help but think of slaves being transported from Africa. Though there are differences in circumstance, we share the same struggle.

When I arrived at the receiving prison for all transfers, our chains were removed once we were within the barbed wire fence that held in a harsh reality unknown to the outside world. A Black man I knew said in frustration, "Damn! Too much chains!" When they removed our chains one by one, the sound of rattling shackles filled the room. I turned to him and said, "They could put chains on our bodies, but they could never put chains on our minds." He smiled, knowing where that quote was from.

I was then assigned a cell made of bars, like a cage. I walked into the cell, and the bars closed behind me. I put my stuff down and introduced myself to my celly. As I stood in this cage, I reached out to grab the bars to remind myself of where I was. In that moment, I felt an overwhelming need to be free, a need for true liberation for all of us.

Later, my celly and I were talking and he shared a story that spoke to me. It was about a bird held in captivity. When the owner, his mom, first bought the parrot, she clipped its wings to prevent it from flying away. She repeated this as the wings grew back. The wings were clipped so many times that, eventually, the bird didn't try to fly anymore, so she stopped clipping its wings. She had conditioned the bird to accept its own oppression.

I will never get used to this. As I look around at this environment, I see everyone walking around, existing within a structure that is designed to keep us down and ignore our potential. This system has manufactured the consent of the men who accept it and are used to it. They've bought into the very system and culture that oppresses them and, in turn, they perpetuate this oppression. I remember walking through a segregated yard: separated by color, race, and gang affiliation, knowing that these men were ready to push the line and fight each other if those lines were crossed. In here, we tend to see each other as the enemy, without truly recognizing that we are not the ones who have placed the chains around our necks. But I can't fault us for our complacency. Maybe our eyes haven't fully opened yet.

Human beings aren't meant to be in cages. Like the bird, I know I'm not meant to be in this cage. They can put the chains on me, try to strip away my humanity and clip my wings, but I'm always gonna try to fly.

Asian Shame - An American Stain
Franklin Lee

Four years ago, in November, I entered my own personal purgatory. I was led down a hallway to a small and dark concrete room. It measured just six by nine feet, and a locked gate blocked the entrance. The lock slid open with a loud clank, and I walked inside.

The room was dark and contained the barest of essentials: a steel sink and toilet, a metal bunk bed that was bolted to the floor, and two thin sleeping mats. The plaster walls were cracked, revealing old layers of paint: puke green, rust red, and a sickly yellow that might once have been off-white. Some of the layers probably contained lead.

To make my bed, I unfolded a starched sheet and a black blanket of questionable cleanliness. Then I climbed onto the top bunk. The last occupant had left a souvenir taped to the wall—a picture of an ocean sunset clipped from a magazine. Beneath it, he had scribbled a bit of scripture, from Phillipians 4:8. "Whatever things are true, noble, just, lovely, of good report," it said, "if there is any virtue and if there is anything praiseworthy—meditate on these things."

Outside the cell, I could hear the roar of laughter and hundreds of conversations echoing in every direction. The sound reminded me of the Mad Hatter's tea party in Alice in Wonderland. Staring at my paper scrap of sea and sunset, I attempted to drown out the chaos. This was my first day in San Quentin State Prison.

San Quentin is in the North Bay, just across the water from where generations of Chinese immigrants came to the United States. They began to arrive during the California Gold Rush, hoping to earn money they could send home to their families, and they labored and died while building railroads.

In the 1900s, an immigrant detention center was built on Angel Island, in the middle of the San Francisco Bay. Families were torn apart, separated by gender into cramped dormitories. The government interrogated the Chinese, trying to determine who already had citizenship, so they could cap the flow of immigrants. With no access to paper, the migrants carved poems, letters, and stories of personal struggle into the wooden walls. The hope was that one day someone would discover their sad fates. Some families never learned what happened to their loved ones.

My grandfather was among the lucky ones. His father had already established dual citizenship in Hawai'i and paved the way for him to come to the States. Later, he would bring his wife and 13-year-old son—my father—from China.

Growing up as a Chinese American, I lived a double life. I was not quite one or the other. My white peers shunned me for my "slanted eyes" or "pug nose"; they called me "Ching Chong China Man" or "Ah-so"; they called me "too smart" or "bad driver."

But it is not in my "Asian nature" to lash out. I am and always will be an outsider, even to Asians. They look at me as "whitewashed" or "ABC," American Born Chinese. I have difficulty rolling my dialect as quickly as my Chinese brothers, and I would rather eat a hamburger than white rice. I grew up believing that I did not fit in anywhere.

That first night in San Quentin, I lay awake in my bunk, listening to the late-night encore of "San Quentin Idol." Contestants tried to out-rap one another with their own "hard-core gang" lyrics. Afterward, across the rotunda in the other block, I could hear the rallying cries of blacks, whites, and Mexicans shouting out their good-night roll calls. How had I ended up being drafted into this army, locked away in one of the worst places in the world?

The next morning, I marched down the tier with the other inmates, through narrow corridors and descending stairs, into a dingy, stained, raucous chow hall. The food was barely edible. Suddenly, I even missed the taste of white rice. In prison, everyone sits at the same time. Everyone gets up at the same time. Everyone walks at the same time. You are just a number in blue, required to comply with any whim or command of the guards. Talk in line, you get yelled at. Hands not behind your back, you get yelled at. Walk out of line, you get yelled at. In San Quentin, you are nobody, unless the guards or other inmates provide you with some unwanted honorific.

In the Asian culture I have known, honor is everything. Living without honor is a fate worse than death. I remember stories of Japanese men who disgraced their family's name and committed hari-kari, or ritual suicide. I remembered hearing that, in China, a daughter who had shamed her family was shunned or beaten.

This made a painful sense to me when I was escorted through San Quentin for medical and psychological interviews. Asian staff members seemed to avoid me with special distaste, as though I had the plague. All eyes would disconnect from mine, and I walked in bitter silence. I was not white. I was not Asian. I was not human.

Who is a typical Chinese American? A student with a 4.5 GPA. who becomes the next successful doctor or entrepreneur? A computer genius or savvy engineer? A lousy driver who sings karaoke every Friday night, dining on sushi and dog? A master of kung fu and piano? I have none of these traits. My family members are not "crazy rich Asians." My parents struggled to make a living. I never had straight A's, and I did not become a doctor. The only typical thing was that my parents owned a generic Chinese American restaurant, and I was that kid doing homework at the far table.

When you look at me, what do you see? Do you make your mouth wider to articulate each word, in hopes that I understand you better? No need, my English is fine. Maybe you pull your eyes at the corners to make fun of me. I had an argument once with a white inmate who stated I must not be full Chinese because my eyes slant the wrong way. Maybe you compare your skin to mine, to see if I am dark enough to know what racism is. When I fill out forms, I am not white, black, or Mexican. I am "other," even though the world is populated by more Asians than any other ethnic group. Asians are still forced into the margins. I feel that I am nothing but a marginal person.

One day, I stood in the prison yard, looking out over the bay, watching the ferries go by. Like most of the inmates, I wore a white tee shirt and boxers during our three-hour yard time. After 21 hours of confinement, we craved fresh air. But on this particular day, it started to rain. There was no shelter, no overhead covering, just the freezing rain pelting me in my boxers. The guards above us watched from the enclosed tower with their rifles.

In prison, the whites hang out with the whites, the blacks with the blacks, Mexicans with Mexicans, Asians with Asians. The misplaced hang out with the "paisas," nonaffiliated Mexicans, usually the ones who speak little to no English. To mingle with another group could lead to an act of violence. Like packs of wolves marking their territory, the clans do not cross boundaries. The whites' TV, the blacks' table, the Mexicans' equipment time—everyone has their place. The percentage of Asians is small. I am one of the unlucky ones. An Asian without affiliation does not fare well.

In prison, every step, every action, every reaction is scrutinized by everyone. If you are not in prison for drugs or gang violence of some sort, then you are looked upon with suspicion. The pecking order is murderers on top, with snitches and sex offenders on the bottom.

At 150 years old, San Quentin is America's oldest continuously run prison. It is a sad testament to the stain of incarceration. During the year that it was my home, I witnessed stabbings with homemade shanks and gunfire from guards. I watched strong, tough men attempt to hang themselves or slash their wrists. I heard the sound of cockroaches skittering across the walls and floors. In the darkness, rats fed upon whatever they could scavenge.

When I was 13, I visited my father's home village in China. Even in Chinese cities, I felt culture shock. My father's village—which was two hours from the large city of Guangzhou—was like a stone in the pit of my stomach. We traveled through rice fields and flat farmlands on a narrow, unpaved road to get there.

When we arrived, I saw a small community of wooden shacks. The one belonging to my father's family had two rooms: a bedroom for six, separated by a curtain, and a main room with a small, portable sink, which served as kitchen, dining room, and living area. There was no linoleum or carpet or wood floors, only dirt, and the light source was a shoddily rigged light bulb dangling from the ceiling. This was what my father had left behind so I could have a better life. Looking back, I know that I broke my father's heart. I know that when I came to prison, his hopes that I would have a better life died.

One day, I will go home, wherever and whenever that may be. First, I will serve at least a dozen years, bouncing between prisons all over California. When I get out, most of my family may be gone. I am still trying to determine whether that matters. I have lost my identity within the judicial system, but I will continue to look for myself. I will always carry my Asian shame, like a scarlet letter, but I will not look back.

All I have is the future.

SHU

Tautai Seumanu Jr.

In the shadows of the tomb where grown boys loom,
Hope…is nowhere.
Wanting to connect.
Wondering if I'm missed,
Wondering…if anybody cares.
I felt my loneliness answer…whatever.
Still, my heart reaches
For fragile fabric of being released.
Slowly, I sink into the belief that no one is thinking of me.
Despairing, sitting here inhaling recycled regrets that filter in from other cells.
Damn, am I still that orphan kid?
The one determined to be there for his drug addicted friends?
Allowing loyalty to become a curse
Knowing they'd kill me, if given a reason,
Still I dive head first in an empty pool
Hoping for substance to embrace my conviction
But subconsciously…I knew…I knew.
Fuck, I even dread admitting that
I envy the coffin for serving its purpose.
Housing the one who'd be missed and is loved…I know I'm not.
But here I am,
Consumed with feeling irrelevant
Questioning my current road.
Sadly… I won't veer off.
Distracted by the steps echoing down the tunnel
As it gets closer.
Decoding eyes welcome another fool to the demon's lair.

He sees me and I feel… Nothing.
I'm hallowed
But I don't know why.

Lying back on this concrete slab, might as well be metal.
I'm wishing for something… I'm desperately wishing for anything.
I silently lay here while my tears release my screams.
While fading…hope whispers…who would visit my tomb?

But then I got your letter.

The Non-Designation Paradox
Douglas Yim

The social dynamics of the California Department of Corrections and Rehabilitation (CDCR) prison system are baffling for someone looking from the outside in. The system has attempted to accommodate inmates such as sex offenders, gang dropouts, and informants by creating Sensitive Needs Yards (SNY) to protect them from the general population (GP). What wasn't anticipated by the administration was the huge influx of SNY inmates from GP due to rigid politics that have been enforced by general population inmates upon other inmates. The booming SNY population has created administrative problems that waste the system's resources due to having to provide various services for two separate populations and doubling up on unnecessary spending. Recently there's been a rollout of yards being converted into non-designated, or program yards that does away with inmates being classified as either SNY or GP. In theory, this is supposed to weed out the bad apples and throw them all into a basket that is referred to as a non-program yard. Program yards are where both GP and SNY inmates are integrated while getting along with each other and "programming," but this is where my story will show that a paradox exists.

Around November 2018, I arrived at the Correctional Training Facility (Soledad) from Mule Creek State Prison (Ione). I was experiencing some anxiety when I got there because I was coming from a prison viewed by many general population inmates as the bottom of the barrel. Mule Creek is the place where snitches and punks (LGBTQ) commingle, if you ask a prisoner who's with the yard politics. Mule Creek is a SNY, and I ended up there because I was in a mental health program. After discharging from mental health, I was transferred back to a general population yard, and CTF-Soledad is where I was headed. I knew CTF's general population yard had politics amongst the inmates, so I was nervous.

"Do you think they'll trip?" I asked my friend Nate before I left. It was the night before my transfer, I was sitting at the ball court conversing with Nate and Joe. Nate and I were born a week apart from each other in '79 and share the same birthplace, New York City. We had become pretty good friends six months prior. He was a Puerto Rican who spoke with a heavy NY accent. I'd lost my NY accent after moving to California at the age of 12.

"Nah, the Asians are pretty chill, yo. At least they were when I was there," said Nate. He had been at CTF prior to coming to the enhanced outpatient mental health program like me. We were both GP inmates at a SNY due to being mental health inmates.

This other guy, Joe, a short, buff Puerto Rican, had a different opinion from Nate. "Man, those Asian guys are gonna say you're no good since you were here and you didn't take off on a chomo. Then you're gonna roll it up after you tell the COs* you have safety concerns," said Joe. Nate could sense I was experiencing some anxiety, so he reassured me, "You got nothin' to be worried about, kid. You'll see when you get there, son."

After arriving at CTF, I was confined to quarters while waiting to go to the classification committee. The yard was on lockdown due to a riot amongst the Mexican gangs, so the program was shut down. My celly was an old Korean grandpa with a long white beard and long hair going down his back around his bald head. If Yoda was an old Korean dude, he would've been this celly. The strong scent of garlic, fish, and chili in the cell reminded me of the funk I'd smelled at my grandma's in Flushing as a child. "Stay away from cellphones and drugs." That was the advice he gave me in Korean. It was like when Yoda told Luke to avoid the dark side. This OG was giving me decent advice, and I acknowledged it.

While I was watching *Jurassic World* on the prison channel from the top bunk, this Asian guy with glasses and a baseball cap came to the window of my cell door. He signaled for me to come down and talk. The cell had an awkward setup, so stepping off of the bunk was uncomfortable. We'll just say he introduced himself as Tom. Tom looked like he could be my distant cousin. It was nice to see a fellow Korean.

"What's your name?" Tom asked me.

"Doug," I said.

"Are you Korean?" he asked me.

"Yeah. You?" I asked Tom. I knew he was Korean from his facial features. He had the distinctive extra-slanted eyes common with Koreans.

"I'm Korean. Where did you come from?" Tom asked me.

The anxiety started to settle in because this was when I had to say I came from Mule Creek and I had been programming around snitches and sex offenders for the past six months. I was hoping that Nate was right and the Asians weren't tripping.

I looked at Tom with as nonchalant and brave a face as possible.

"Oh, I just came from Mule Creek. They sent me there cus I was in the mental health program," I told Tom while keeping cool. I went on to explain a bunch of unnecessary details.

Tom was emotionless as he shook his head up and down.

"Mule Creek?" he asked me. If I was telepathic, I would've read his mind as saying, What the hell are you doing in general population?

"Is that going to be an issue?" I asked Tom.

"I'll be back later," he responded. Tom walked off into the dayroom area. I hopped back on my bunk and continued to watch the movie on my small TV that was tied to the ceiling. There was pandemonium on-screen with humans being eaten and snatched away by pterodactyls. I was worried about Tom and what the Others would say. I imagined they would want to remove me from the yard. I imagined Tom stabbing me with a homemade ice pick. A Cambodian kicking me in my nuts. A huge Samoan jumping on my head with state-issued boots. That asshole Joe might've been right, I thought.

I felt some anger underneath my anxiety. I just wanted to do my prison term with minimal bullshit. I wasn't a sex offender or a snitch witness that had put someone in prison. I had never dropped out of a gang. I had ended up in the mental health program because I was serving a 75-year sentence, and it was a lot to handle so I'd asked for help. The unfairness of prison yard politics was depressing to think about too.

Tom came back to my cell the next day. This time he caught me in the middle of reading my Bible and praying to Jesus that I didn't get jumped by the thugs on the yard. I was hoping that it was all good for me to stay on the yard. Was God watching over me?

Tom didn't look too happy to see me.

"Are they tripping, dude?" I asked Tom.

"Why did you go to Mule Creek again?" Tom wanted to clarify.

"Mental health," I said.

"Some of the older homies are saying it's not good that you came from Mule Creek," Tom said in a low tone through the crack in the door.

"What?!" I responded. Those motherfuckers, I thought.

I became defensive. "Man, I'm not a rapist, child molester, snitch, or any of that, bro!" I told Tom angrily.

"The Koreans ain't trippin', cus we all just wanna go home. Some of the older Asian homies are used to the politics being a certain way," Tom explained.

I explained to Tom how the administration was making statewide changes to integrate GP and SNY yards together. I forewarned Tom, saying, "This yard is flipping to non-designated soon. You know this, right?"

Tom nodded in acknowledgment.

"Look, dude. I'm not with the yard politics, and I just wanna do my program. I don't cause trouble, and I don't want any crazy shit happening," I said.

Tom might've thought I was insinuating that I was going to do something crazy. He was probably concerned since I was mentioning all of this mental health stuff.

"The last thing we want is anything crazy to happen, so let's figure out what we can do so things can be cool," Tom said bluntly.

I was defensive. "I respect that you guys are political or whatever. I'm not trying to be blindsided and jumped when I get off orientation status. So tell me if I can't be here, and I'll bite the bullet, then tell the COs to roll me up if that's the case," I said.

Tom nodded his head. "I'll be back," he said, then disappeared to the dayroom.

I felt pissed off and rejected by my peers for no good reason. It was like I was being looked down upon for something that was out of my control. For all I knew the guy that was dictating this decision was some drug addict who'd be shooting heroin in some alley if he was free, and this idea made me even more upset. This was some straight-up bullshit.

Tom came back a few minutes later after speaking to some mystery Asian dude and gave me the bad news.

"It's not good for you to stay, so you should do what you gotta do so you can leave," Tom said.

I got one last piece of info in before this conversation ended.

"This yard's flippin' soon, and there's going to be some sex offenders and snitches coming over here. Those OGs that said I can't be here are going to have their hands full when that goes down. I hope they stick to it and get what they have coming," I told Tom. It was a toxic thing to say, but I had to get it off my chest.

"It's just politics, Doug. You know how it is," Tom said sorrowfully.

"I know you're just trying to program and go home, so it's all good. I'm not going to fuck that up for you, Tom. I'm not here to start shit," I said.

It was futile to say anything else because there was no way I could change the minds of those bastards who said I was no good.

"Thanks for being cool about it and not creating problems, Doug. I appreciate that," Tom said. I could tell that he was a decent person trying to go home from prison. We might've been cool if I had stayed. "No problem. Take care and God bless," I said, and then nodded goodbye.

Tom disappeared.

After I packed up all of my personal property, I explained to Korean Yoda that I had to go. He didn't understand the politics and why Mule Creek was so horrible. He didn't even know mental health services were available in prison. He didn't have a clue about how I'd tell the COs I had safety concerns. I spent only three days as his celly, but I'd end up missing Korean Yoda and his ancient prison kimchi recipe. Joe that asshole had been right, I thought.

I spent four shitty days in the hole waiting to see the classification committee. It sucked pretty hard. There were bars instead of doors, so I could hear my neighbors conversating loudly during the day. They were some dudes from a Mexican gang who came to the hole after a riot with another Mexican gang. They were the ones who had put the GP yard on lockdown. Listening to them casually talk about senseless violence made me think, what the hell is up with these guys and their bullshit politics?

I've made my fair share of mistakes. I killed someone and got a life sentence for it. I know there should be some form of punishment for my crimes, although I also think there shouldn't be extra bullshit added on top of the time I already have to do. Apparently a lot of prisoners feel the way I do because I've discovered that many inmates on the SNY are regular inmates who just want to do their time without prison politics.

I think CDCR wants to save money by doing away with the two separate designations for inmates. Being able to assign inmates and officers with more flexibility saves them a substantial amount of time and money. They label them program yards, but the paradox or contradiction in a non-designated "program" yard is that while it intends to foster positive programming, it actually creates situations of conflict that result in bullshit.

I'm on CTF North Yard now, and it hasn't flipped to a program yard yet. I left Central Yard due to politics, and now I might have to deal with confronting those same politics again when general population inmates transfer into North Yard, which is a Sensitive Needs Yard. I'm nervous about that because I've been staying out of trouble and am on the trajectory to parole someday. Anything to ruin my chances of paroling someday is what I try my best to avoid.

I guess all I can do is read my Bible and pray to Jesus to keep me away from trouble.

Voice of the Voiceless
Ricky May

My life is similar to many API BROTHERS who've been sentenced to decades in prison. In 2006, I was 16 years old when I committed my crime. I was apprehended at the age of 17, and at 18, I was tried and convicted to spend 27 years in prison. At the beginning of my prison sentence, I was on the brink of destruction. Sentenced to what seemed like a lifetime, I became a caged beast.

After years of violence, prison politics, and the monotony of idling and merely existing, I came to a crossroads while serving time in segregation. Battling with my thoughts, I wondered, What am I living for? What is my purpose in life? Is my life destined to be lived behind these four walls?

The day I was incarcerated was a blessing in disguise. The men who have been deemed by society as menaces and no good are the same men who've helped change my life. My API BROTHERS helped plant the seed and nurtured me to grow into the man I am today.

The mainstream perception of prison is that it's solely violent and chaotic. That perception is outdated and superficial. Many fail to see our personal growth and development. Many fail to witness what we are doing to help each other and the work we do to unite, educate, empower, and pass down our traditions and the culture of our people as API BROTHERS.

However, prison continues to be a storage facility for those deemed unworthy and is not a place of correction or rehabilitation. The growth and development we gain is due to our own personal motivation, not the institution of prison itself. The motto remains "Lock them up and throw away the keys"—a harsh reality, but nevertheless very true.

I write for understanding.

Yes, we have made selfish choices, many with devastating consequences. But do our bad choices make us any less human? Do we not deserve equality? Do we not deserve a chance for redemption? Or will we live forever with the stigma of being a criminal?

The API ideology in prison has helped change the mentality of many serving time, including gang members. We as API BROTHERS have adopted this ideology, and as a result our communities are safer. We must work to be united as APIs. I know firsthand the positive effects it has had on my community. There's yet to be a killing amongst my people over gang and turf wars in almost a decade.

This is a testament to the power of the brothers serving decades in prison. They have made it their responsibility to help change the vicious cycle of gang violence. You often don't see the transformation and power of API BROTHERS from the inside, who strive to change one life at a time from behind these prison walls.

Organizing for Freedom:
An Interview with Charles "Bula" Joseph

Please share briefly about the process where you were transferred from CDCR to ICE. What were the most difficult parts of that transition?

I was granted parole and eventually released from CDCR on May 17th, the day after my birthday. I woke up at 4:00 a.m., made sure I had all my stuff that I was taking with me, and made a cup of coffee. And I waited and waited. Finally they finally called me and said, "Come on down with your property." All I had was paperwork - my legal paperwork - and pictures, letters, and my guitar. The only thing I took with me was my guitar, because my guitar had all signatures. It was signed by everybody I know. All my brothers in there, they had come together and had a little party for me and signed my guitar. I had a bunch of signatures on my guitar. That's why I can't play it to this day, because I still have to figure out how to seal all the signatures on there.

So they called me to R&R, and I get to R&R, and I'm excited! I'm ready. I knew my mom was coming to pick me up - my mom and my wife. But, they never called me to go out to the front. And then this truck pulls up in the front. So they pull up, and I had a couple of Mexican guys in the holding tank with me and they start saying: "La migra, la migra!" And I'm like, "What, what's going on? Where am I going?" The guys that got out of the van just replied, "You'll know when you get there. We can't really talk to you. I can't really answer your questions." They didn't even wanna tell me if they were ICE, or where I was going to be taken to. So they cuff my hands and my legs and escort me to a van. I was taken to Sacramento from Solano. And then they put us all in the van again and we drove all the way down to Bakersfield, and we waited there for a couple of hours. And then they take us to Mesa Verde at 3 am. Man, it was messed up. We waited there in that holding cell in Mesa Verda 'til like

6 in the morning, before they found a place to put us. Then we walked up the stairs and I went into the dorm.

Being in CDCR, I was always in a cell, I had never been in a dorm setting. So I had my own space. I was able to clean my own cell. I was able to clean the bathroom and keep things the way I wanna keep them. When I went to Mesa Verde, as soon as they opened the door and I walked into the dorm, it's just.. The smell - the first thing that hits you is the smell. 'Cause there's so many people. I came later on to find out that there was a hundred people in that dorm, in that one room setting. And it was... the smell. That's one thing that hit me first, was the smell. I'm like, Aw man, this is not cool.

And I had to go use the restroom. So I go in the restroom and - again, the smell. And I'm looking around and I'm like, Where's the soap? Do they give us soap? I just remember turning the water on and splashing water in my face. I went to use the bathroom and it was like, Okay where's the toilet paper? And then they told me, "Oh you have to ask the police. The police have to give you everything." So I asked the little guard and he said, "Oh, we don't have soap, but I can give you toilet paper. Here's half a roll."

I didn't know how long I was going to be there. You go to prison and it's like, You know this is what happened, this is what you got, this is what you have to do. In ICE, I didn't know why I'm here or how long I'm here. After a while, I started talking to more people and I came to find out there was a lot of people in there for years. And I'm like, Why? Why are you here for years? We beat our case, and then the government appealed on us and lost a second time. So we're in this ninth circuit where we're moving along and we have to go and fight again. There was a guy in there, he was there for 6 years. The guy who got out with me, my buddy, he was in there for 4 years. He was from Jamaica. He got out the same day I got out. But I was in there for 11 months when I got out. He was in there for 4 years fighting, fighting hard. He just came from prison also. And there were a couple of people in there just... indefinitely. They don't know what the hell is going on.

You mention that even when you first arrived that there was a connecting of a small community of others. Just in ICE in Mesa Verde, how did diverse groups of people from different backgrounds,

from different languages, come together to take collective action to try to improve conditions at Mesa Verde when you were there?

California prison is very segregated. And so when I went to Mesa Verde, it was very similar. There were divisions: you had the "others" and Hispanics from Central America, South America. And then you have some of the gangs that came from prison that are also there. The one thing that was different that surprised me was there was this white guy that came to Mesa Verde and he was lost! He's from England. He actually just came from prison! The whites in prison are very like, Oooh, you know? They're off on their own. So he comes to prison and there's no category for white guys in immigration, right? So then the white guy is an "other" in immigration. At that time, when he arrived, I was already there for a few months. I was able to go talk to him and see where his mind frame was at. And he was like, "Man, I'm just trying to get home. I'm just trying to go through." And I told him, "Man this is it. You're cool, you're an 'other.' Come over here. We over here is good." We're not tripping on all that nonsense, you know? Everybody here is just fighting and trying to get to somewhere better; they're trying to get home. Either guys are trying to get home, or they signed their deportation and they're waiting just to leave, get on a plane and leave. But most of the guys were fighting, most of the guys were fighting to get back to their families. It took him a little bit to reflect on it, but he took to it really easy, you know? And he was better.

Was there a particular collective action that you can speak of? You mention there's the legal fights. Were there any types of fights or struggles that happened in your dorm or throughout the detention prison?

So while I was there, COVID had hit. I used to get up early and watch the news everyday. And so we'd just see COVID and it's spreading. I started having conversations with the guards in December 2019 and January 2020 just to see if they had anything that they were going to implement anything or if there were any updates. And they also told me, Nah, nah, nah. And then the conversations progressed to, What are you guys going to do? It's coming closer! And then we started hearing, Okay, COVID is in California. And then I talked to the guard and the guard said, "Nah, it's not in our county!" One of the ICE officers replied, "Why are you worried about COVID? You guys are safer in

71

here. Why would you wanna go anywhere? Stay here, you guys are safe." It just showed me where their mind frames are at, they don't really care about us. Then I had a conversation with the warden. I was asking him all of these questions and he said the same thing. He said, "You guys are safer in here. You guys have nothing to worry about."

And so after those communications, I realized that this wasn't going anywhere. I was watching the news and it kept talking about risk factors: people with asthma, people with heart conditions. And so I begin to write something out. I wrote this letter addressed to the officials - ICE officials - all those in power. We came up with this list, this list of about 40 people out of the dorm that had medical conditions, risk factors. And at the same time, Interfaith Movement was connected through my case and they were assisting me with my case, especially with getting me an attorney. We had access to video calls and Gala made an appointment to call on a video visit. I told all the guys: "Listen, they're gonna do the recording. I want everybody, everybody, back here. Let's show unity. Everybody stand here while I read this letter out loud. And then after we're done reading the letter, I want everyone to come say hi to the camera. Let people see who's in here." The call came in, she pressed record, and everybody was behind me while I read the letter. As soon as I was done reading the letter, I moved out the way and all my bros they walked around, everybody walked by. They said hi, did a peace sign, or some kind of gesture. Everybody was so excited because they were getting calls from their family like, "Oh, we seen you on YouTube!" And so the warden finds out about this video and he shuts down the video calls. And then he blocks Galatea from ever calling me. When we made the video, that was really for relief. First of all, they didn't have anything in place. We need safety! We need cleaning supplies! Oh my goodness, the bathrooms were so filthy. We've been asking for cleaning supplies since I've been there. It was a big struggle just to get cleaning supplies. And then, on top of that was relief from deportation. We've been to prison, we served our time. We were deemed releasable by CDCR on parole. We were granted parole. Parole is supervision. It made no sense to me. How was I granted parole by CDCR and then you not grant me bond or bail?

And then, I was fortunate to get in contact with Centro Legal and they assisted me a lot. They started taking calls from people. They said, "Can you make a list of all these people? Can you get them together and put them on the call so we can talk to them and take down their case and information?" So I had lines of guys. I said, How much time do you have? I was talking to Priya at first and Priya was like, I want you to call Susan. So one phone would be Priya, and there would be a line of guys on one phone back to back handing the phone off while Priya is taking down their information and writing down their health risks. And then I go use the other phone and I call Susan and Susan is like, "I'm ready, get it started!" And I have a whole line on this phone and Susan is taking down information. So it was about three phones and three different attorneys taking down information.

There was no change, though. All of that, and there was no change. More conversations, still nothing changed. And then me and the guys, we got together, and we were just like, We have to do a big demonstration, we have to do something big. And so we planned a demonstration on the yard. I also sent out a letter and it was able to be sent out and passed on to the women's dorm also and they planned a hunger strike.

Then, the day before the demonstration I had just found out that I was finally granted release. The day of the demonstration comes and I make sure the whole dorm goes out. Me and my buddy, we rally up everybody. Everybody out the door, the whole dorm outside. So we all go out and we do a sit-in on the yard. A warden comes down to speak to us and so he's talking to me: "I know you're the one doing this, Mr. Joseph, but you have been granted release. These guys are still going to be here." He's talking to me like that. And I tell him, "Listen man, it's not a me thing. Everybody can speak for themselves. My brothers can speak for themselves." I told the guys I can't be the only one talking because if it's just me who knows what's happening and speaking up, then they would just cut the head. They'd just throw me in the hole and then this whole thing would die. So everybody started learning what's happening, what are we standing for, what are we doing. And it spread like wildfire because everybody was ready, you know? So then everybody started speaking when the warden came out. My buddy from Honduras stood up and started speaking in Spanish! And I'm like, "Listen, it doesn't matter what language we speak, we all have the same concerns. This is real. You're taking it lightly, you're not paying attention to us. You're not giving us what we need. You put on this video about proper handwashing for us to watch, but you don't even provide the stuff we can use in the video to practice proper handwashing." And so the warden got frustrated and left, then he finally came back at the end and he threatened everybody. He said, "All you guys are getting write-ups. This will go to your judges. Your court cases will be affected." It was all bad. So the guys started getting turnt up. They were ready for violence right now 'cause now there's been threats.

So we walked into the field and got to the middle of the field and then we created this circle. At the same time, this drone flew overhead. And by some miracle, when the drone took the picture, the formation on the ground was a heart-shaped formation. Nobody even spoke a word. There wasn't any instructions. It was just so natural! By the time the picture was captured - and I've seen the picture! I didn't even know it was heart-shaped 'til I seen the picture. It was a trip. And when we were outside, we also heard at the same time, it was Kern youth abolitionists. They were outside the gate across the parking lot chanting. And we could hear them! They were saying, "Libertad! Libertad!" And so when the guys got out there, this sparked much more of a fire 'cause now they're excited, you know? They started chanting, "We want freedom! Libertad! Libertad!' We're all saying the same thing and then we all came together and said, "Okay, we're all gonna chant together. One, two, three! Libredad!" In one voice. It felt so powerful, man. It was amazing. I was real fortunate to be part of that moment. It felt really good. I was really happy, man. This could all be our doom, but we're here and we know the cause is just.

It was escalating and there was potential for violence. So I talked to the guys and a few of the main heads, we came together and we had a conversation and we decided that we would go back in and continue the movement by going on hunger strike alongside the women, because the women were on hunger strike at the moment. So we went in. And we went on hunger strike from that day, so the tenth. April 10th. April 10th, 11th, 12th, 13th. That's four days. And I was pretty much hallucinating by the fourth day. And then they call my name for release. I couldn't believe it until I was actually outside. I was just like, Wow. I made it out. April 13th, 2020.

What are your lessons learned from this experience of organizing in ICE around hope, around power, around solidarity, around organizing?

First by understanding that we are all suffering the same thing, we all have the same sufferings, and we all have the same needs and desires and wishes for the future. The biggest thing I had to face was trying to help people understand not to be afraid. And a couple of people asked me, "Hey, you shouldn't go out there. You could mess it up." Because that's what my attorney told me. He said, "You could mess up your release. Whatever you do, be careful, you could mess up your release." And my buddies also had that thought: "Hey, maybe the price is too high for you. You already have the chance to be released. You don't have to do this." But then it made it even more important for me to do it because there's so many other guys in there that are not going to be released. They've been there for years fighting. And me asking them, Hey, let's do this action. Let's do this not just for us, but for the future. People have to know that this ain't right and there has to be a moment in time when people have to stand! And this is our time. We have to stand, man. It's so easy for us to be violent. But what does that do? That's not going to do nothing. All that's gonna do is mess us up even more, put a worse stereotype on us, people look at us with more violence now. We just have to highlight the truth. It could affect us, and I couldn't guarantee that it's not gonna affect anybody's case. But at the end of the day, it had to be their choice: are you willing to, you know? This is for the future: your parents, your children, the community members, your nephews and nieces. This could help them. Even if it doesn't help you, this is beneficial, this is important. This is what it is and this is our time. We are here now. And so I don't think it really hit them, how serious I was about the calls I was trying to push for until I got my order of release. Then they see me on the day I was there. When I rallied everybody up, they were like, "You're going?!" I'm like, "Yes. I'm going to be out there." And then it kind of motivated them even more.

I was released April 13th. The hunger strike ended on April 13th, the day I was released. A couple of my buddies called me from in there and I told them to keep going, you know? This is not the end. Keep moving forward. Keep moving together. It's essential. And so they kept in touch with the attorneys, and the attorneys started helping them all. And eventually, the population decreased in Mesa Verde, partly due to the widespread danger and impacts of Covid. At the moment, the population decreased from 400 hundred people - because there's four dorms in there: A, B, C, and D. And every dorm has a potential of a hundred people in there. That's four hundred people. So the population decreased from 400 to 52 people! It capped at 52 people. That's big.

A lot of the people I knew inside have been released since then. I mean, some of them have found me on Facebook and they're just like "Boola, boola!" They don't even speak English but they can say "boola" though! It's a blessing, it makes me feel good just knowing that. They're my brothers.

Some have been deported. Especially a lot of my Cambodian brothers there. They had deported them. A lot of them. Also my Punjabi brothers too, they got deported. But they got tired also. They were there for years, and they got tired and just signed. And they left.

Today I am reunited with my family in Sacramento, but I am still under ICE supervision house arrest. I can't even cross the street being on this ankle monitor and house arrest while my immigration case is still pending.

Through my experience in ICE, I learned a lot of things. The establishment itself - that place, that location - it wants to keep people separated, you know? It loves the division because that way the people can't unite against a simple cause. So that's better for them. But all it takes is extending the hand, and communication is essential. Even if it's through different languages, the need is the same. It doesn't matter if we come from different places. If you're suffering in one situation, you can guarantee the next person in there is also suffering. We're all suffering and we just haven't communicated that to each other to see how common it is. So we all have a common cause, we're all suffering under one thing regardless of our division, separation, belief, faith, whatever it may be.

Outside/Inside Power
Adamu Chan

I work in the education department here at San Quentin as a tutor for people who are working to attain their GED. Three days a week, there are students who come from UC Berkeley to help tutor in the classroom I work in. They are mostly young, 18 to early twenties, men and women of color, liberal arts majors. From the conversations that I've had with many of them, they are driven by a desire for social justice and equity, especially in the area of education. Patrice is a young black woman who is an aspiring writer. Her youthful optimism and energy is inspiring and refreshing. Last week at work, I was talking with her about one of my writing projects, listening intently to her feedback and critiques. The banter was very casual and friendly, the type enjoyed between colleagues or peers. "The students at Berkeley don't even understand the things that you are writing about and discussing here, and that's a problem," she said. We were in the midst of discussing the complexities of identity and its potential in redefining social activism when my "correctional supervisor" came into the room, his body tense and bristling. He said in a loud voice, "Don't be telling these guys your first name. It's just not a good idea." It should be noted that this supervisor is neither a correctional officer nor a prison administrator, but rather a GED teacher employed by the education department here at the prison. Like many of the employees here, he wields his power in ways that seem to signal a lack of power in other areas of his life. To clarify, the "guys" he was talking about were people like me, incarcerated and wearing prison blue; his statement was directed at the two young women from UC Berkeley that were in the room. I was suddenly aware of a familiar sinking feeling about safety, and prison, and my place as a prisoner. Was the implication here that to know each other on a first name basis blurs the lines between inmate and civilian, educated and uneducated, human and inhuman? It seemed a strangely indirect threat—him performing his masculinity in an aggressive way, while simultaneously alluding to the potential danger in my masculinity. I remember the students' reaction, a robust silence and shameful acquiescence that came from being forcefully reprimanded by an authority figure. Was it his tone, his age, his gender, or was it that his directive, that felt violent, suddenly brought us all back to the reality of prison? I couldn't tell. Something about casual human interaction seemed to threaten the legitimacy of the established power structures in that room and his position within them.

Situations like this have become all too familiar to me, as I live in an environment where I am constantly at the receiving end of aggression—both passive and direct—mostly from people who work here. Prison is a space where, because boundaries and relationships are so clearly defined, and resources so scarce, and because the threat of violence is ever present, the spectre of power is clear in every movement, every interaction, every breath.

Ironically, I've heard numerous times from volunteers who come into these incarcerated spaces that they've "found themselves" in prison, that they've never felt so seen or heard, or felt so safe. Many of the volunteers are women, and I've been asked many times why men on the outside can't be like the men in here. The answer to this question has much to do with power, roles within the existing power structure, and how those roles are enforced.

I think it's important to acknowledge my own role in participating in a world where women feel unsafe and objectified, and are subject to violence and harm. Additionally, the women in my life have made clear to me that safety from gendered or sexual violence is an urgent and ever-present concern for them, and that experiencing men who are nonthreatening and who listen to them can feel like a revelatory and rare experience. In that context, I can imagine why it would be enticing to come into a world where people all of a sudden hang on your every word, laugh intensely at your every joke, and are meticulously attentive to your personal boundaries.

I can remember a particular instance where I was at an event put on by the prison that was attended by both outside volunteers and incarcerated persons. I was standing at the entrance greeting people as they came in and was at the same time engaged in a conversation with two women. One of them was a college professor here in the prison college program whom I respect greatly for her political and social insight. As people started to trickle in, I commented to both of them that none of my fellow incarcerated peers, who were entering the space and walking past us, even acknowledged my existence, so eager were they to say hello to the two women. The professor chuckled and turned to the other woman and said, "Isn't it nice to be seen? We're so invisible on the outside." As they laughed in solidarity with one another, I couldn't help but feel injured by the irony of it all and wondered if they could recognize how invisible I felt in that moment. I came into an immediate and focused awareness about how power was operating in that room. In a place where I was forced to wear a uniform, and be called an inmate, and be heavily policed in my interactions and expressions, these women were feeling seen in the full spectrum of their humanity.

I've heard in classrooms, self-development groups, and passing conversations stories from women about experiences ranging from domestic violence to workplace bias to mansplaining. These experiences obviously reflect the serious sexist/patriarchal norms that persist in our society, but they also make me reflect on the viability of San Quentin as an oasis or sanctuary from those systems of oppression. I've heard people joke that San Quentin is the safest place in the Bay Area for affluent white women. But in every joke, there is some truth. San Quentin is a place where they don't have to face our blackness or our masculinity or the ugliness of economic inequality in ways that they may out in society, because of the way that all expression and interaction is policed here. Entering this place as a savior absolves one of the guilt and fear that one may have on the outside. You are here to help, and that's why it's "safe."

The issue is how these "safe" conditions are created for some at the expense of others and why this seems to be a paradigm that we are always working from. For example, why do some of us have to live in a world of police and prisons and surveillance, while others live in the normative safety of whiteness, of maleness, or of hetero-ness? The safety and visibility that outside people experience here is at all times established by the gun towers circumscribing the grounds of this institution, the presence of guards, of handcuffs, batons, and the merciless shadow of the parole board. These mechanisms, to most volunteers, are not always visible, because of the nature of San Quentin's "rehabilitative" atmosphere, but they are ever present and always at work. But they are also created by the way in which prison deprives the incarcerated person of truly human interaction—in which people meet as equals and are free to share ideas, experiences, and connection. People who are incarcerated hunger for that type of interaction, the type that validates one's humanity, one's value to the world. The problem is that within the incarcerated space, the incarcerated person will always inhabit the space below. Even the most honest efforts tend to replicate the dominant/subordinate dichotomy.

Reflecting on this makes me think about the ways in which I have, in certain places and times, inhabited the space above—because I was a man, because I had lighter skin, because I was skilled or educated, or had money. I made decisions and behaved in ways to maintain power in those instances, like ignoring or harming less powerful people. Those who are in dominant positions are not taught to recognize power's embedded permutations, and thus I was led to believe that what I was doing was good and healthy, and certainly in accordance with the norms and rules that I had been taught. I believed that power was derived from some quality that was innate to me, and was not just situational, or arbitrarily awarded privilege. The fact that I was a man was natural, and the behavior that flowed from that was natural as well. Those natural rights, I thought, afforded me the privilege of seeing women as interchangeable sex objects fashioned for my gaze and, at times, treating them as such—not seeing them as inherently equal or deserving of equal treatment, equal attention, or equal safety. But I was lacking the awareness in those moments that roles within power are transposable; although I was in the dominant position in one space, a slight shift rendered me the slave. Looking back, I can't help but think that regardless of which position I occupied in those situations, it is clear now that my humanity was distorted by power, and that the true person that I am exists somewhere outside of these structures of power.

I think it is important to state that my experience here in prison has included glimpses of how people can relate within equality—moments in which I have collaborated and shared with people, both outside and inside, in trying to redefine the old modes of dominant/subordinate relations. Whether it was through the arts or through sharing our stories of trauma and healing, these experiences, although fleeting, have given me hope that we can learn to live and communicate outside of our current patterns and definitions of power, recognizing our position within existing structures and co-creating safety together without hierarchies of human worth, to be neither colonized nor the colonizer.

Since the incident with my supervisor, I have seen the young woman from UC Berkeley one more time. Upon seeing me, she called out, addressing me by my first name, "Adamu!" Then, as if the brutal realization of where she was suddenly set in, she lowered her voice and said, "Hi." I explained to her that I planned on writing about our experience in the classroom, in lieu of a conversation that seemed to suddenly be impossible and fraught with anxiety and wariness. She replied, "I can't wait to read it. I'm going to write something too." With that we parted ways—I, with the knowledge that I'd most likely never be allowed to read what she would write. Outside, a light rain began to fall.

R.O.O.T.S.
Rhummanee Hang

It was my first time behind prison gates
I didn't know what to expect except
I was there for ROOTS
Restoring Our Original True Selves
A program for Asian Pacific Islander men
To delve into ethnic studies

After a series of ID checks
I trekked across the yard
Picturing hardened faces
And curious stares
I didn't imagine
The way I'd be *greeted*
By so many people
in the sea of blue

In the San Quentin classroom,
I was taken aback
All these API faces
Some Latino, some Black
And *every person*
Introduced himself
Shaking my hand
Then I met a man
Who was there since ROOTS began
He was *familiar*
Khmai refugee child

Teen years wild
You wouldn't have guessed he'd been inside
20+ years with his smile

So we sat in circle
And recounted stories
I knew too well
Colonization then war making times seem the *hardest*
To be 2 and travel through
Roads of human carcass
Parents living with PTSD
Passing it on intergenerationally
Unknowingly
Parents who worked all the time
Who found comfort
at the bottom of bottles
Or coped in casinos
The frustration
Of growing up poor
The anger of being bullied
The sadness of so much loss

The story of folks from Laos
Was the same with Kampuchea
Was the same with Vietnam
Was the same of those born
in Thai and Filipino refugee camps
Head nods in the circle
Some tears
Confirmed it all resonated
And in that circle
I didn't see people who committed crimes

I saw remorse

I saw men who understand the harm they caused
And the harm they experienced

I saw brilliance

Folks who could break down systems of oppression
Better than hella grad school students I knew
I saw empathy
I saw transformation
And in that circle
We continued to heal

Together

"We must stand up against these oppressive systems and dismantle them until the walls crumble and the cages are ripped apart. That means it will take all of us to free them all, and for me, that means using my voice to protect the most marginalized communities, sharing my journey as part of healing dialogues, and holding sacred the priceless gifts of love and compassion bestowed upon me by my community."

— *Ny Nourn, "From Surviving Systemic Violence to Liberating People from Prisons and ICE Detentions"*

BEYOND PRISON

Art by
Chanthon Bun

Captured Moments
Tautai Seumanu Jr.

Gazing at every captured moment you've lived.
My heart rides a roller coaster with every flip,
One after another.
My heart exhales the emotional buildup
Wiping the streaks from my face
As my smile says…

I love these pictures.

Oh my goodness, look at your girls!
Looks like she was about to smack her sister
With her arm cocked back but stopped
When she saw you with the camera.
She had that 'Oh Damn' look on her face
And, her hair was everywhere.

I love that picture.

Look at you and the family all dressed up in your Sunday best.
You guys look so good and aunty still think she stylin'.
What, nobody stopped her
From wearing that bright yellow sombrero ass hat.
White flowers around the brim, she's F.O.B. fo' life.
Yeah I know, that's aunty.
Ha! Ha! There's a stain on your dress.
Truthfully sis…that's why I really

Love that picture.

Okay, stop the press and no one moves.
Look at yoouu! Watch out now!
You're, Miss I Own This Moment.
Miss, This Is My Time.
Smilin' your big crazy smile.
Bravo, Bravo! Congratulations to you.
My little sis, Miss Cap and Gown.
Ms, My Diploma Means I'm Smarter Than My Brothers.
That's right sis, I'm squad leader number one cheerleader…
Go! Sis! Go!… I got yo' back.
But you know, you know I'm mom's favorite.
Still, while holding these pictures
I'm consumed by a humbling feeling of happiness.
My jaw clenches while tears ease my heart.
I am so very…very proud…
I'm so proud of you.

I really, really love these pictures.

Oh shit! Check you out.
Smilin' from ear to ear
On your big girl vay-cay.
Lookin' like an uptown girl
In New York, New York.
Obviously you're having a blast.
I'm so happy for you.

That picture is awesome.

Wow…look at you.
Holding these pictures proves that God is beautiful.
Sis, you're gorgeous.
I wasn't there but…I'm crying like I was.
You're a stunning bride. No camera tricks at all.

Your wedding photos captured the meaning of happiness.
My god you're beautiful sis
You look so happy…so beautifully happy.
You know me, you know I believe in family protecting family
That's why I had to give 'em the talk.
Still, with no words my tears say it all…

I adore those pictures.
I love…every beautiful moment.

I've accumulated pictures throughout the years
And with every flip, weight is added to my heavy heart.
While my smile struggles with holding everything together.
Loving the moments in your journey
I silently cry for lost moments not shared
And uncontrollable laughter that becomes an inside joke.
Sitting here flipping pictures like a slide projector
Grinning slightly and wiping my nose
While my heart tries to breathe.
My pride wrestles with regret
While being mesmerized by moments that captured your growth
Making you the beautiful women I'm so eager to meet.
My little sisters became young women
Then found love and then gave life to love.
Every photo I have…immortalizes… all of your smiling eyes.
Damn…I missed so much…I miss you all so very much.

So snap on and click away,
I love the windows of your life.
Snap away and capture everything.
I'll slightly grin… wipe my tears
And slowly flip from one… to another.

I can't wait for your pictures.
I know I'm gonna love every moment.
So close your eyes and think of me… can you see me?

Can you see me smiling and crying...holding your pictures?
Now that is a picture of a proud brother
Smiling and saying...

I love... I love that picture.

Something in Common We Trust
Michael Manjeet Singh

Leading up to the concert, people would often ask, "Is Common actually gonna perform here?" Then on the day of the concert, as I came out to the yard at noon for my insulin shot, I saw a concert stage being set up. Inside the trailer of an 18-wheeler, there were huge speakers. It was super-amazing just to see the stage, because I hadn't seen one since the start of my incarceration in 1996 when I was just 21 years old. (I'm excited just recalling it!) At approximately 6:45 p.m. my housing unit was let out to the yard, after a security "pat-down" by the guards. I wheeled my wheelchair around the track. At first, I was limited to staying on the concrete. I could hear really loud thumping music and see hazy concert smoke and lights. Me and another disabled (blind) brotha stood at an ADA (Americans with Disabilities Act) table. The grass field quickly grew crowded.

Suddenly, an Inmate Disability Aid (IDA) worker came and wheeled me onto the grass, much closer to the stage. The show started and the audience exploded when Common, dressed in all black with a hoodie, energetically hit the stage. The noise got even louder when he started rapping! As I watched the show, I kept forgetting I was in prison, but I was jarred back to reality each time I saw a clique or crew walk in either direction. I've seen a lot in my 22 years of incarceration, and even on the street (free world) there are a lot of fights at rap concerts. Being disabled, I felt especially vulnerable.

But back to the stage—Common's energy radiated in a truly positive fashion! Leaving no race out, Common gave shouts of love and respect to us all: Asians, Blacks, Latinos, Native Americans, and Whites. I truly felt the impact of his songs' positive messages. No concert has ever made me think so much! It was an invitation to introspection, and like Scrooge in A Christmas Carol, I saw my past, thought about where I was now, and even dared to dream about the future.

Please understand that as an LWOPer (a person serving life without the possibility of parole), dreaming is something I never do! This experience at the concert almost caused me to shed tears. In prison, it's taboo to expose vulnerability because it's always exploited as weakness. The Youthful Offender Program (YOP) inmates were loudly chanting, "Common, Common, Common!" YOP had gotten special time with the entire Anti-Recidivism Coalition (ARC) crew and Scott Budnick, founder of ARC, before the concert. Dudes I would've never thought was bobbin' they heads front to back and wavin' they hands back and forth! All races were intermingled!

Prison is a place where there's always gonna be people who don't like each other. Despite the fact that there was coverage in the darkness and it was incredibly crowded, there were no stabbings! No one snuck into the middle of the crowd to slice someone's throat. There wasn't even one fight! I was stunned that nothing happened! A true anomaly! I was so happy—because it proved that for one night, all of us could come together and hope for a better future. This was more important than for any one person to attempt something in the name of retribution or for the lure of false prestige and artificial respect for unnecessary violence that a gang gives members who "put in work for the crew." The concert was awesome. In between songs, Common reached out with positive messages for us all: he told us it was our future and that he was there for us (I really felt his authenticity). Common came down from the stage and hugged brothas of all races standing at the barrier. Back onstage, he asked, "We got any rappers out there? Who can rap?"

Suddenly, helped onto the stage was an Asian (Hmong) brotha, about 5½ feet tall, with four strands of braided hair, two on each side, same length as his height. Then the DJ started playing a beat and the crowd got hella "hyphy" (hyped up). The inmate rapper known as Cha-Zilla missed the starting beat, and the crowd simultaneously said, "Awww!" Then the next beat came and Cha-Zilla was on it! Spitting lyrics as the beats flowed, he held onto the mic with one hand and rhythmically moved the other to the enunciation of his words! It was hella cool! Common reached out to all of us and created a truly positive atmosphere. Even the staff got in on the act, nodding their heads and recording the show with cell phones in the air! It was like that for almost the entire duration of the ARC concert—no one wore blue (inmates) or green (correctional officers). It felt like we were one and without any racial barriers!

In my 22 years of incarceration, I've never seen or experienced anything like it, and I mean that! Hope was inspired, unity was formed. In between a song, Common introduced his fellow performers. To my best recollection, they were as follows: DJ Ace; Julian, electric guitar; Abdul-Karim, background singing sista; and Phil, drums. Common also talked about MCs he grew up to like KRS-ONE, Big Daddy Kane, Rakim, and recent greats Tupac, Biggie, Jay-Z, and a few more. After performing a few more awesome songs, which transferred more of Common's energy to the crowd, he finished with shout-outs to other agencies helping us and our families—Initiate Justice, the Ella Baker Center, Gina Clayton-Johnson's Essie Justice Group (all organizations I've come to know through my correspondence with them over the years)—and shout-outs to us, SATF (Substance Abuse Treatment Facility) "E" yard, Warden Sherman for approving the concert, and all the staff there. Then Scott Budnick got on the mic—he told us he was with us and described Chicago's finest Windy City native and how hard Common had fought for us at the state capitol in Sacramento to help pass laws that would give us a chance to parole earlier. Afterward, former "lifers" of all ethnicities who now work for ARC spoke to the crowd, each saying his name and how much time he had served": "I did 22 to life!" "I brought 30!" "I fought a 25 to life—y'all know me!" There were also two sistas, one Black sista—"I did 20 years!"—and one Latina sista—"I did 25+ years (on an LWOP)!" I could not believe it, a former LWOP was onstage! I'm currently an LWOP! Then ARC executive director Shaka Senghor got on the mic and gave us love, telling us he was working hard for us and knew, as a former lifer, what we were going through—"I've worn your shoes and I won't forget!" My night was an experience of positivity and hopefulness, from the atmosphere of the concert (during which I experienced a past, present, and future emotional journey) to the night free of violence—inside a prison, with convicted felons, at a rap concert, no less. I gained hope for the future with me embracing my skills just like the many former lifers in the current force of ARC. Common said "Peace Gods!" to all his brothas- us.

The whole experience energized me, empowering me with hope, and made me come to a realization that under my "state blues" is a guru untapped!

Note: In the days leading up to this event, I kept hearing about the Youthful Offender Program's sponsors and all the countless hours our counselor put in to ensure this whole ARC event would actually happen. Correctional Counselor I DeLa Cruz counsels and assists us to strive for better and greater things; he can break down lyrics and actually reach us inmates. I've made it a point to mention him because most staff become CCIs for the weekends off and/or lieutenant's-level pay. DeLa Cruz teaches us how to turn stumbling blocks into stepping-stones. That's why ARC's show happened here, at SATF.

Fighting the Power
Michael Manjeet Singh

Books called it THE GREAT MIGRATION, but people aren't birds
Yet we fly in flocks & also remain lonesome doves
So do crows & many of them equal a murder
Birds of a feather, flock together
And the worst of vultures kill us all little by little with each passing day

With oppression & by smoke bombs, metal batons and O.C. Pepper spray
The penitentiary is a place with fair weather friends
This ain't no game, cause our wings are tied or clipped
That's why so many take black tar[9] with a syringe and have dipped
Because for some it's better and easier to inject their veins with dope
Instead of to fight the power and system with their brains fueled with hope.

To talk to yo' "Dear Mama" cost way more than a dime
The guards charge you a thousand for a clapper[10], then try to take mine
'The Man' bringing you the coke to 'blow'
Wears a green jump suit & calls himself a C.O.
Ironically, the very next day, you get 'called' for a U/A[11]
In my world of prison, this is just your average and typical day
My humanity is NOT up for negotiation
That's what has messed up this entire state of the U.S. Nation!
Young lions SINGH (SIKHS), grow up in and are a Mother's pride
It's when you get older, that you see the system has truly lied.

---

9 Black tar: heroin
10 Clapper: cell phone
11 U/A: urine analysis test

From Surviving Systemic Violence
to Liberating People from Prisons
and ICE Detentions
Ny Nourn

For anyone to survive nearly 16 years of incarceration immediately followed by ICE detention and the threat of deportation would be nothing short of a miracle. With 16,000 Southeast Asian refugees in the United States currently facing deportation, however, these conditions are far from uncommon. Witnessing and enduring domestic violence, surviving the conditions of both prison and ICE detention, finding freedom from incarceration, and organizing for the freedom of immigrants and refugees has not only prepared me but shaped me into who I am today: a freedom fighter working in the movement to abolish the carceral system.

In 1978, my mother, barely 18 years old, escaped from Cambodia during the genocide that killed over 1.5 million of my Khmer people. For weeks, she fled on foot, swam through muddy rivers, and walked over land mines, before finding safety in the neighboring country of Thailand. While living in one of Thailand's refugee camps, my mother met my biological father, who abandoned us shortly after I turned one. The memories that I have growing up in the refugee camp for the first five years of my life are foggy, but I can still distinctly remember the loneliness, fear, and sadness that I felt, and the physical pangs of cold and hunger. In 1985, my mother and I arrived in the United States as part of the largest refugee group of over 1.2 million Southeast Asians. And like many Southeast Asian families that came between the late '70s and early '80s, we had difficulties resettling in the United States without adequate resources or access to social services, such as mental healthcare and language accommodations.

Growing up in San Diego, California, was difficult for me because my family and I moved often, and because of the constant moves, I had problems adjusting and focusing in school. To add to that, my life at home was consistently unstable because of the domestic violence that I was exposed to by my mother and stepfather. I can only imagine that as refugees, they were both unable to deal with their own personal traumas, which ultimately carried over as anger and bitterness that seeped into their relationship with each other. Unfortunately, their abusive relationship was my only model for what relationships should look like, and I became trapped in an abusive relationship of my own as a result. At 17 years old, I met a guy twice my age over the internet. In the early stages of our relationship, he was constantly showering me with affection, and we were inseparable. Shortly after, though, he started to become critical of my physical appearance and choice of attire, and became jealous of me spending time with my friends and family. His words went from light teasing to deliberately hurtful remarks that made me doubt my own self-worth and question whether I was worthy of being loved. In public, he was respectful with everyone he encountered and gentle with me in front of others. Whenever we were alone or out of public view, however, he would verbally put me down and yell at me. His promises of love and a future together turned instead into a cycle of lies, verbal abuse, and manipulation in an attempt to control my life. At the time, I was unequipped to recognize the red flags or warning signs of an abusive relationship, and I had no one to confide in about what I was experiencing. During my senior year of high school, shortly after turning 18, I became involved with another person while still in that abusive relationship. My abuser found out about the person, and out of rage and jealousy, forced me to confront the person with him. He then shot and killed that person. I feared that if I tried to tell anyone about what he had done or if I tried to leave him, he would find out and kill me and my family. Despite the fact that the physical abuse worsened after that, I remained silent for three years. I was finally able to break free from him after a co-worker encouraged me to report the murder to the police. But instead of being protected from him, I was arrested, charged, and convicted for the murder my abuser had committed. The police, prosecutor, and judge all believed that I was responsible for my abuser's deadly actions and blamed me for his behavior; they didn't care that I was not the one who had taken the victim's life. Sadly, domestic violence survivors like me, people of color from poor economic backgrounds, are often criminalized by the legal system that is supposed to protect them. Instead of being supported, survivors are punished for actions done in self-defense and/or are blamed for their abuser's behavior. Survivors are sentenced to an excessive amount of time in prison and often end up serving anywhere from 15 to over 25 years before they are eligible for parole. At just 21 years old, I was sentenced to life without the possibility of parole (LWOP), which meant I was going to spend the rest of my natural life behind barbed wire fences.

In 2003, I was sent to the Central California Women's Facility in Chowchilla, California—the largest women's prison in the world. After being separated from my family for the first time, over five hundred miles away in an unfamiliar place, I fell into a deep depression that was accompanied by thoughts of suicide. After spending some time attending a domestic violence support group, however, I started to take in what the other survivors were sharing. I soon realized that the personal circumstances that had led to my conviction were not isolated or even uncommon. It was their first time in prison, as it was mine, and they were all serving lengthy or life sentences. The survivors' backgrounds were strikingly similar to mine, particularly the abuse and trauma we had experienced prior to the events that led to our convictions. These support groups were the starting point of my healing journey. I relied on these survivors not only for my personal healing, but also for our shared hope for freedom. It was beautiful how we supported each other's growth and the belief that our court sentences were not final, that one day we would be free and reunited with our loved ones, and that society's judgment of us as monsters and villains was only their opinion, not ours to accept.

As the years went by, I continued to challenge my conviction while I was incarcerated. In 2008, an appeals court finally gave me an opportunity to be one step closer to freedom. The courts granted me the opportunity to appear before the parole board because they had recognized that the circumstances of my conviction were directly related to the abuse I had received from my abuser. I ended up being resentenced to 15 years to life, which meant that I'd have a chance at freedom if I could present my case to the prison parole board. Knowing that I could possibly be paroled one day, I continued to work hard on my healing and growth, preparing myself for life outside the walls with my family and community. During that time, I had many personal accomplishments, including becoming a substance abuse mentor and obtaining certification in paralegal studies, as well as becoming a fitness and health coach. I also earned a college degree while continuing to do volunteer work with the California Coalition for Women Prisoners (CCWP), a grassroots organization whose goal is to help challenge the excessive sentences and inhumane conditions for women inside California prisons. A few years before my parole hearing in 2015, however, a friend of mine told me that I would be facing deportation despite being a permanent resident. I looked into it and received a response back from the Asian Law Caucus (ALC) in San Francisco telling me that despite being a child of a refugee parent and green card holder, my conviction would make me deportable to Cambodia. I was beyond devastated that no one had told me this, not even my attorney at the time I was arrested. But Anoop Prasad, an attorney from the Asian Law Caucus, visited me in prison and shared with me that there was immigration relief available to stop my deportation. But that chance of relief was slim. Nevertheless, I knew I had no choice but to fight for my freedom and try to remain in the United States with my family.

In January of 2017, I appeared before the prison parole board and was recommended for parole. I was told that it was unlikely that I'd be deported to Cambodia. Because I knew better than to believe what the parole board told me, I consulted Anoop, who informed me that Cambodia was accepting deportees, and only a Convention Against Torture (CAT) claim would provide me with protection from being deported. Although there was about a 50 percent chance I'd be able to win a CAT claim, that was still better than nothing, and I tried my best to keep hope alive inside of me. In the months before my release, I couldn't even look forward to leaving prison because an ICE agent had already visited me to tell me that they were going to arrest me on the day of my release. Thinking about being arrested by ICE left me overwhelmed with feelings of fear and anxiety. And in May of 2017, after 15½ years in prison, on what was supposed to be a day of celebration, I was shackled by the leg and waist in chains by a private security guard contracted by ICE, who then escorted me into an unmarked white van. I was temporarily detained in a freezing-cold holding tank at the Fresno ICE field office for a couple of hours before being put in another unmarked white van and driven nearly four hours to the Yuba ICE detention facility near Sacramento.

Yuba County Jail was a coed facility that also rented space for ICE. It was a place that could only be described as a suffocating and filthy dungeon, filled with hopelessness and despair. The first evening I was there, it gave me flashbacks to when I was first arrested, but this time, it seemed like my time in prison had made me more aware of the horrendous conditions I was now dealing with in Yuba. I was housed in a pod, a dormitory-like setting, with about thirty other women. Like me, they were all facing deportation without any idea if they would ever be reunited with their loved ones in the United States or if they'd be facing potentially much worse and more unsafe conditions when/if they were deported. We had to share two toilets, two sinks, and four showers that were lined up side by side with only a flimsy piece of green plastic that was supposed to be a curtain for privacy. If we were lucky, we got an hour of fresh air per day. There were two phones in the pod, and they were in constant use, as many of the women were attempting to contact an attorney or a legal aid organization for help with their immigration case. Unlike in state court, people are not automatically assigned an attorney in immigration court, so very few can afford to hire their own immigration attorney. As a result, many people end up representing themselves in court, which ultimately seals their fate for deportation because immigration judges only see people for what they have been convicted for, with little interest in stopping their deportation. In my case, I was fortunate enough to have my community by my side every step of the way, particularly when the #FreeNy campaign was launched for me after I was transferred from prison to ICE detention.

Despite the support I had, my time in detention was difficult, due to the conditions inside and the constant worry that I would be deported to Cambodia rather than reunited with my loved ones. I'm grateful that I had more hopeful days than days filled with anxiety and fear. I was able to stay connected with my community through letter writing, phone calls, and visits from members of Survived & Punished (S&P) California—an organization working to fight for the freedom of criminalized domestic violence and sexual assault survivors—and the Asian Prisoner Support Committee (APSC)—a grassroots organization helping to provide direct support to API immigrants and refugees—as well as countless other individuals who encouraged me to stay hopeful. My community's endless support also inspired me to make my own commitment to do organizing work to help free survivors, immigrants, and refugees from prison and ICE detention.

On November 9, 2017, after six months in ICE detention, and after a total of 16 years and one day of incarceration, I was released on bond and was finally reunited with my family and community. Being released from ICE detention was only possible because my community raised over $10,000 to make sure my bond would be covered. That evening, as I was waiting in the jail lobby for my attorneys Anoop and Melanie to pick me up, I was consumed with a mix of excitement, relief, and nervousness, knowing I wouldn't have to spend another night sleeping in detention and wouldn't have to sit behind a plexiglass window waiting for my visitors to come see me. Since being freed, I still think about how grateful I am that I can open a door without fear of it being locked behind me, that I can ride a bus without cold and heavy leg and waist chains gripping my skin, and that I can enjoy a meal with my family and friends without a guard standing behind us, watching our every move.

After my release, I became a first-time resident of San Francisco, and have had the opportunity to explore its beauty. I've now traveled up and down California, and have even taken a few trips to the East Coast. In 2018, I accepted the Yuri Kochiyama Fellowship offered by the Asian Law Caucus. The fellowship was established to empower formerly incarcerated API immigrants to lead advocacy-bridging movements against prisons and deportation. The fellowship gave me many opportunities to share my story as well as the stories of other incarcerated immigrants and refugees facing deportation, including numerous occasions to lobby local and state elected leaders, and to speak at hearings, events, and rallies at various college campuses. Through this fellowship, my voice was heard at the State Capitol, in Washington, DC, and in front of multiple prisons and ICE detention facilities. I also became an organizer with S&P to aid in the release of criminalized survivors, while also serving as a council member with APSC and doing anti-deportation work. In addition, I continued to volunteer my time with CCWP, where I was involved with the #DropLWOP campaign. Following the completion of my Yuri Kochiyama Fellowship, I was offered the community advocate position with the Immigrant Rights program at ALC, where I would continue to provide support for immigrants and refugees in state prisons and ICE detentions, advocate for pardon campaigns for many Southeast Asian refugees, and help build on immigration policies to stop ICE transfers of people from local jails and prisons to ICE detention.

Despite the fact that I had been out of ICE detention while on bond for nearly three years and had developed a solid relationship with my community, I was still concerned that ICE could arrest me and begin deportation proceedings at any time. Then, unexpectedly, one morning in June of 2020, the governor's office informed me that the governor had granted me a full and unconditional pardon. A pardon meant that I no longer had to fear being arrested by ICE and that I could remain in the US with my family and community. The pardon also gave me a lot of relief because I knew I could continue to organize and fight for the freedom of people in prisons and ICE detention.

After experiencing decades of violence in interpersonal relationships, prison, and ICE detention, I'm grateful that I've survived these traumas—but knowing that many others have not is heartbreaking. It's also heartbreaking to know that so many Southeast Asian refugees have been exiled to countries where they have no family or community ties. Seeing the irreparable harm that incarceration and deportation causes people fuels me, along with many other freedom fighters, to continue the movement to liberate community members and reunite them with their families. I know that as long as the carceral system exists, it will only perpetuate harm and continue to cause division among our diverse communities. We must stand up against these oppressive systems and dismantle them until the walls crumble and the cages are ripped apart. That means it will take all of us to free them all, and for me, that means using my voice to protect the most marginalized communities, sharing my journey as part of healing dialogues, and holding sacred the priceless gifts of love and compassion bestowed upon me by my community.

The Awakening
Bao Vu Nguyen

I enter the prison yard with shame draped over me like a soiled rag. The behemoth metal gate slams shut, emitting a thunderous boom as of a coffin being closed. The imposing concrete walls, rigid and stern, loom over me. Barbed wire coils along the ridge, threatening to string me up.

The yard is a stitched blanket of cracked pavement, dirt, and dried patches of grass, a ravenous quicksand gobbling up anyone caught in it. Vigilant guards sit perched on gun towers. Their hands cradle Mini-14s at attention. This is it, I realize this is the oblivion where I'll spend the rest of my wretched life. Gone and forgotten from the free world. Not a vestige of me remains. My hopes and dreams are mirages, dissipating like smoke into the ether. I am chained with self-doubt and ignorance. I speak wordlessly to listeners without ears. Only the abyss hears my cries. I walk the yard, a condemned man among condemned men. The quicksand pulls at my feet. The more I struggle, the faster I sink. I give up, and let it swallow me.

In my final hours, as darkness closes in on me, out of that sphere of consciousness, that engine of thoughts, comes a lifeline. The thread that comes with responsibility and accountability is there for my salvation. I only need to take it. Self-doubt stays in my hands. Ignorance clouds my mind. The furnace whence my thoughts arise is unlit, devoid of any intelligent spark. I have nowhere to go and no one to turn to. Then comes the realization, slapping me in the face: I've hit rock bottom!

In this moment of crisis, my mother—goddess and creator—comes to mind like a vision giving me strength and courage. Words she spoke to me throughout my life now ring in my thoughts. "Be good," she says. "I will always be there for you." Her tender voice and warm smile encircle me, hugging and shaking me. Memories of her embracing me when I was young and when I'm in prison fill my vision. I am cocooned in her arms as she holds me tightly. Heat radiates from her golden heart. Its pulses are as strong as solar flares. My skin is singed from the memory of her touch. My heart is engulfed in her loving flame. Shocked from my reverie, I grab hold of the line.

As the sun emerges over the horizon, my mind clears and I realize, for the first time, that I have choices. That choice, that omnipresent entity, is the key to unlocking the secret of life. To choose is to live, and I can choose my destiny—I feel renewed and invincible, and am awash with potential. I see things from a new perspective. My vision crystallizes, and I see how foolish and selfish I have been. No longer will I be the victim of my circumstances, nor will I be led by other people. Sitting around won't help me. I refuse to let idleness and ineptitude be my masters any longer. From now on, knowledge will guide my path, self-improvement will be my compass, and motivation will be my drive.

I pull myself out of the darkness. I am a seedling that is seeing sunlight for the first time. My arid mind thirsts for the shower of knowledge. I embark on a road of self-awakening. It begins with drops of black ink on a white sheet of paper. Emotions and feelings that I couldn't enunciate are expressed loudly on blank pages. Happiness, sadness, and all the sensations that encompass the human experience manifest in the heroes and villains in my stories. Anger screams while sorrow sobs, and I scream and sob through them. My verses, however, lack intelligence. I am a bell with a bandaged tongue.

My teachers, scribes and scholars from empires long gone, have made their bed in the ancient earth. Their teachings remain in sacred parchment, stored in the library of mankind and passed down through the ages.

I devour Shakespeare for breakfast and guzzle Poe for lunch. The former teaches me the sonnets, and the latter teaches me the macabre. Dante teaches me more about heaven and hell than all the saints could. Marcus Aurelius teaches me about life. I am entertained by countless poets and writers who play and cajole me into the night.

The quicksand solidifies. The walls and barbed wire seem less menacing. With my goddess spurring me on, I charge the day and wrangle it with my bare hands. I am awake.

Spiritual Quest
Nou Phang Thao

In the year of perfect alignment, high in the Hmong mountains, an echo of joy vibrates through a cottage in Five Clan Village. Grandma works with skill and precision in a bedroom lit by candles. She catches Lee Sang Pao's firstborn son, cuts the umbilical cord, and wipes the child clean of birth fluid. Grandma hands the baby back to his mother, Xee. She enters the living room and informs her four sons the baby is a boy. They admire the child in his mother's arms.

Sang Pao asks his youngest brother, Ger, to do the honour of naming his firstborn son. "I would like to name him Nou Bly." Lee Ger bends down to pick up his nephew. The child kicks his leg, knocking the blanket—along with his uncle's hand—backward. Nou Bly pushes his uncle's finger with a microcosmic hand. The family is taken aback by the infant's liveliness. "The child dislikes you, Ger," brother Lee Hua says. "Maybe the boy doesn't want the name you gave him. Step aside, let me give it a try." Leaning closer, his eyes make contact with Nou Bly's. The newborn shakes his head. "No!" Hua jerks back in horror. "Hlob Pao[12], what's the matter with your son?"

Lee Sang Pao asks Grandma to bring the candle closer, and the illumination reveals his son greeting him with a smile. Sang Pao offers his face to the boy. Nou Bly clenches his dad's cheeks. He pinches it into a smile and places a small peck on the tip of his father's nose. "Son, stop scaring your mom, grandma, and uncles." The baby releases his father's face.

Pao hurries to the living room. He stands before the ancestor's altar and chants the words of ancient shamans. "In this year of perfect alignment, ancestors, what blessing does the day bestow upon me?" Pao picks up a wooden cup. It is unsteady in his hands. *I have done this hundreds of times before*, he thinks. *Hmmm,*

---

12 Older brother

strange. Maybe I am tired. He pours the water on the ground, retrieves fire from a nearby stove, and places the flame on top of the water. To his amazement, the water dances around the flame. Then, both elements rise and hover above the ground.

Lee Sang Pao returns to the bedroom. "The elements of earth, air, fire, and water are in strong harmony," he announces to the family. "We are blessed with a spirit child—he is born with knowledge and foresight. When the time comes, he will be the village's next shaman. My son can formulate thought. It's only a matter of months before he can start talking. Please, do not let anyone outside of this room know of my son's gifts. What happened earlier with Ger and Hua wasn't a coincidence. No need to fear, come."

Sang Pao and the family approach his wife, who is in bed, cradling their son to her chest. Pao takes the baby and kisses his forehead. His son burrows deeper into his arms. As Pao gazes upon such a precious gift, his teardrops sprinkle Nou Bly's silky cheeks. "These are tears of joy, Son, dedicated to helping you become a great man."

Meanwhile, in the depths of the gloomy jungle, an ultraviolet light bursts among banana leaves, casting shadows on living organisms and nocturnal creatures. A four-legged beast lands on the ground with a thunderous thud. The Tiger King inhales a deep breath of misty air, then bellows hot steam from his virile lungs. His ears perk, his head tilts sideways, and his eyes dart back and forth. "Something is wrong. The air on Earth is usually fresh with a cold sting." The Tiger King treks slowly along the jungle floor, leaving prints on the muddy trail. He sniffs the ground. The area to his left is pungent. The Tiger King pounces forth, following the smell of a demon.

The demon pulls itself along the jungle floor with stick-figured arms, guts spilling from an underdeveloped body. It can sense life-forms on the other side of the mountain. Its cringeworthy face has one deformed side and a bulging eye on the other. Since escaping from another realm, the demon has not fully gained strength. It needs the spirit of a human body to recover.

Lee Sang Pao jolts from a deep sleep, chills running down his spine. He strains to his right; Nou Bly is asleep in Xee's arms. Pao's spirit detects the presence of a powerful dead spirit nearby. The feeling has never been this overwhelming before. It's his responsibility as village shaman to keep everyone safe. "Maybe the incantation to protect the village is broken." Pao jumps out of bed and darts out into the early morning.

From his home in the third district, where all the villagers have equal access to him, Pao runs past the fourth and fifth districts to the rear village gate. Gasping for air, his mind in disarray, Pao has the same uneasy feeling he had earlier at his altar. But the warding spells that he engraved into the post are fine. *It's better to be safe than sorry*, Pao thinks. He walks along the village fence, inspecting the magic thread woven through it with care. Arriving at the left gate, Pao places both hands on the post. "The living may pass, but the dead can no longer go beyond this point." A small light glows before his eyes, confirming that his spell is holding. Pao's pulsating heart begins to calm.

Beams of light peek through the morning sky. A dense patch of fog descends from the mountaintops. Five Clan Village is a heavenly paradise floating among the clouds; a moment of joy before the day begins. Homes stir with life as villagers get ready to tend to their fields. Whatever shook Pao out of bed this morning is no longer present.

He hums to himself on the way to the rice fields until a large commotion beyond the trees quiets his tune. A group of villagers point to the ground. "There are tiger tracks all over," one says. "There and there." Another person says, "Villagers from other mountains were out hunting. They saw three humans transform into tsov poj nthxoog[13]. They dragged a deer away into the forest." Fear silences the crowd. Lee Sang Pao kneels to inspect the prints. "Six paw prints! What's it doing so close to the village? This demon spirit is what awakened me this morning." Everyone fixates on Pao. He raises his hand and speaks in a soothing voice. "A regular tiger was out hunting near our village last night. Tigers are very skittish and solitary animals. The loud noises everyone makes scared it away."

Xee walks toward the river, where villagers wash clothes. Nou Bly is wrapped in a Hmong cloth around her lower waist and back. She looks over her shoulder

---

13 Tiger ghosts

at his glowing face. He flashes her an innocent smile that lights the world. She moves her shoulders and says, "Coo coo!" Nou Bly's giggles can capture any heart. Xee places a bucket of clothes next to the stream, just past some bushy trees, and keeps an eye on her son as she washes. Nou Bly points at a tree. "It's okay, baby. Mommy is almost done."

Inside a lair in the trees by the river lives something mountain people cannot speak of in the daylight. It crouches on a stump, stalking the road with grey, translucent eyes. The demon ghost sees a smiling baby. When Nou Bly giggles, the thing is filled with bloody hunger. The demon licks its lips. "Yeessss," it hisses quietly. "Capture the baby and trade it with a guardian so I can travel back to the land of the deeaaad." Its fingers intertwine as it thinks of the possibilities.

The dead spirit crawls out from the trees. It's eyes are locked on Nou Bly, whose spiritual aura casts a bright light. The demon inches toward the woman and her baby. Xee looks over her shoulder and peeks at Nou Bly. He is pointing at nothing. "Okay, baby, Mommy is almost done. You can eat soon." The demon, invisible to Xee, picks up Nou Bly and tucks his shining spirit under his shirt. The demon hops back into the trees.

Lee Sang Pao pulls weeds from his rice fields. The sun is at its highest point in the day, and it beats down on his body. He stops for a break. In the distance, a figure approaches. It is brother Toua, breathing heavily. "Hlob, Hlob! Niam Hlob[14] says to go home now! Something awful happened to your son!" Panicked, Lee Sang Pao runs. The soles of his feet pound over rough rock edges. His muscle calves burn. *Just keep moving. I hope my son is okay*, is all he can think. He rips the flesh of his hands on bamboo stalks as he pulls himself up the mountain with reckless abandon.

The front door bursts open. "Xee, where are you?" Lee Sang Pao yells. "We are in the bedroom—come quick. What are we going to do, koj txiv[15]? My handsome boy is unconscious." Pao wipes a bloody palm on his pants before placing it over Nou Bly's precious little chest and listens to his son's heart. Nou Bly is alive. He parts his eyelids. They are pure white. The bright aura from his son's forehead is missing. "Where did you both go today?" Pao asks. "I carried

14 Eldest sister-in-law
15 Husband

109

our son on my back while I washed clothes by the river," Xee answers. "He smiled all day. But when we arrived home, our son didn't respond."

Pao understands. "Nou Bly's spirit is captured, and he is in a trance. I need to perform a ritual to retrieve his spirit." Brother Toua pulls a bench from beneath Lee Sang Pao's ancestral altar and places it in the middle of Pao's living quarters. Brother Ger holds a brass gong. Next to him, brother Hua holds a ring with brass coins in the middle. Sang Pao pours cool water from a basin to purify his body before his journey. He places water on his hands and face. Pao gathers his thoughts, but his heart is restless. "Nou Bly may not be alive."

Hua beats the gong. *Boonng, boonnng, boonnnng.* Six times, five times, four, three, two, one. This pattern is echoed—*chinnng, chinnng, chinnng*—by the brass rings between each gong repetition. Lee Sang Pao stands in front of the bench. Toua gives him a black cloth to cover his eyes, but Pao pushes it back firmly. "Hlob, though we are healers, the red one is to kill spirits." Pao knows the purpose behind his decision. Toua straps the spiritual sword around the bench.

Pao concentrates on the instruments. His breathing is slow, deep, calm. The rhythm of the music vibrates his body. Wave after wave leads him to a heightened state of awareness. His body convulses as his spirit leaves the flesh. The music leads him toward a dim light. The light comes closer, closer. Then, flashing colors and static appear before Pao's eyes. He is unable to step through to the other side; there is a blockage in his body. "Your fear, fear, fear, fear," voices whisper all around him. In the darkness, fear has infected his body with anxiety and uncertainty. Pao realizes he must acknowledge his powerlessness and fear of being a father. This negative force is preventing him from tapping into his power. Pao meditates, and the flashing colors fade. Pao stands beside his body. He can see his brothers beating the brass gong and shaking the brass rings, but he can no longer hear the shaman's instruments.

Pao pulls a leaf from his shirt pocket and blows on it. A huge shadow appears from the sky, landing in front of him. "It's been a while, phooj yoog[16], since we rode together." Pao whistles twice to inform Toua on Earth that he is ready to take flight. Toua hears the signal: "Blaaah tiiaa, blaaah tiiaa!" He moves into

---

16 Friend

110

position behind Lee Sang Pao and lifts him onto the bench. The black stallion approaches Pao, and they are airborne. As they fly over the spiritual realm, Pao searches for the stream where Nou Bly's spirit was taken hostage.

The winged stallion dives, landing on a riverbank. Pao eases himself down. "Show me where Nou Bly is located." Pao blows over the riverbank. Ghostly footprints appear, leading into dense underbrush. Pao creeps, sword strapped over his shoulder, to a thorny tree. The tree forms the shape of doom. Pao clears a slight opening and carefully steps to the other side.

Inside the doom, Pao drops to the ground. His chest thumps against the grass, his mouth is dry. A stump and a tall rock block his view. From behind the rock, a dim light glows. Pao springs to his feet, pulls the sword slightly from its sheath, and quickly steps behind the rock. He hits a twig. *Snap!* He hears quick shuffles and loud cracking on the other side. Releasing his sword back into its sheath, Pao pulls out three rice sticks and a side of raw beef from his shirt pocket. "Nyob zoo[17], I come bearing gifts. Please allow me safe passage?" He steps into the clearing.

Light radiates from Nou Bly's spirit, adding colors to the doom. Pao turns to his son. A huge tension releases from his body. Nou Bly is lying on his stomach, pointing to a far corner. "Do I have permission to enter your home?" Pao asks. "Who goes there?" a deep, raspy voice from a far tree responds. Pao extends the food in his palm and shows surrender with the other. "I am a lone traveler. Can I enter your home in peace to rest?"

The translucent outline of a man no larger than himself takes form as the demon ghost hops toward Lee Sang Pao. Even dressed in a ragged shirt and cutoff pants, the dead spirit is nothing but skin and bones. The spirit points. "Gooo, before I am mad." Pao extends his palm further. "Can we at least sit down and eat a meal together? I traveled a long way. See, I offer you the best food I have." The dead spirit eyes him. "Okay, no tricks! My name is Jay." It stares at Pao. Then, sensing Pao is not a threat, the demon admits its name is really Danv.

"Can I speak freely, without you getting upset, friend?" Pao asks. Danv barely

---

17 Greetings

has the strength to nod in approval. "I am here on behalf of that little boy. His parents are worried about his spiritual well-being. They are willing to pay you a pig and thousands of gold coins." Danv stands just out of Lee Sang Pao's reach. Pao smells a foul odor and feels cold chills coming from the dead spirit. "This food is a gift for you." He lays it on the ground and takes a step backward. Danv's dead eyes barely blink as it reaches for the goods. It places a rice stick and meat into its mouth. "Hmmm, yummm, good." Pao looks in Nou Bly's direction. Danv continues eating from both cupped hands. Through its fingers, it spots sweat dripping down Pao's neck.

The dead spirit lunges at Pao like a frog, hands outstretched. Sang Pao lifts his hand. "Stop." Danv freezes in midair. Grunts escape its throat, but it is unable to move its limbs. "If I release you from my spell, will you harm me?" Danv is frightened. "I will not threaten you! Don't leave me like this." Pao reaches into his pocket and pulls out a leaf. He extends it toward Danv. "Can this demon ghost be trusted?" The leaf stands straight up, revealing the Danv is untrustworthy.

Pao's hands tremble. He lets out a long sigh. Danv screams, "Help, help me!" Pao places the leaf into his pocket and withdraws a tiny wooden bottle. "Help me now!" Danv screams louder. Lee Sang Pao pulls the cap off. "Into the jar." "Noooo!" Danv's voice disappears. Pao places the cap on the bottle and tosses it into the air. His sword zips out and slashes the tiny item into two pieces, which burst into flame. Pao watches the pieces burn on the ground.

Crack! Out of the shadows appears a huge monster with killer eyes, drooling jaws, and razor-sharp claws. Flying downward, the creature swipes his paws. The powerful force swirls in front of Pao as he steps back. The Tiger King chomps his ferocious fangs. Pao can feel the breath of death. He dives out of the way and rolls onto his feet. The beast turns and growls. Shock waves smack Pao's chest and slam him against a tree. The tiger roars, jerking its body side to side. "Argghhh-ooommmm!" The boom of his voice transforms all the thorns, twigs, and tree branches into apocalyptic living limbs. They grasp Lee Sang Pao's arm. With his free hand, Pao slashes the tree arms with lightning speed. They fall to the ground and turn back into twigs. The tiger glares in Nou Bly's direction.

"The boy belongs to me," the tiger snarls. He bounds toward Nou Bly. Pao pulls a brass coin from his pocket, points his blade, and taps it with the coin. Rays reverberate from the blade, knocking the tiger onto his side. The tiger stands up, shakes his head, snarls his fangs, and stalks toward Pao. "Die, shaman!" Pao places his weapon in a striking position and advances full speed at the monster. He swipes at the tiger's head, but the beast is swift; his claws rip Pao from shoulder to midsection. He screams as the sharp claw burns his spirit. Pao presses the brass coin beneath the tiger's jaw, scorching him. Black blood seeps from the opening.

The Tiger King withdraws, moaning in pain. Angry, he whips his tail against Pao's stomach. Pao swings his sword downward and cuts the tail off. The tiger roars and seeks to saw Pao's body in half with its powerful claw. In a swift motion, Pao's blade slices clear through the tiger's paw, chipping a fang. The Tiger King retreats with a low, defeated *meoww*. He hobbles away, looks back at Pao, then jumps into a bright light and disappears. Pao drops the sword and falls to his knees. He grimaces as he touches his wounded shoulder.

Gathering himself, Lee Sang Pao walks toward his son. He takes Nou Bly in his arms. "Spirits, my son is not ready to receive your gifts. When he is ready, we will invite you back." Pao draws X's on his son's forehead, heart, and stomach. The X's glow neon, then dim and disappear. This spell will keep future dead spirits away.

"Blaaah tiiaaa!" The brothers play the shaman's instruments to lead Pao home. They don't stop until Pao, drenched in sweat, finally removes his red veil.

Pao accepts a cup of ginseng tea from Toua to rejuvenate his spirit. He walks into the bedroom where his son is asleep in Xee's arms. Pao places his hands near his son's forehead. "Follow my voice home, spirit of Nou Bly." Nou Bly stretches and opens his eyes. There, a familiar radiant smile.

HEALING

Art by
Gary Taylor

Spinning with the Earth
Kenny Lee

Remembering the summer days in our childhood, a truly beautiful place,
Mountains high and green, they reflect the colors in reality.
Song birds on the wind, trees in concert with the river and its gurgling voice.
Free if we are compassionate, love can break the chains.
Free if we have empathy, true freedom is of mind, heart and soul.
Every year she sleeps, in a place of shelter, in stillness we find peace.
Filled with power we rise, alive, living all.
We are drops of water from the same sea.

Lost & Found
Kenny Lee

In the summer of 1971, I was born into a family of Chinese refugees in South Korea. I was the youngest of four children at the time of my birth: Lana was 12, Lan was 6, and Shung was 4 years old. Due to China's involvement in the Korean War at the time, Koreans had developed a general dislike of Chinese people. We were discriminated against in every aspect of our lives. My family owned a Chinese restaurant in a small rural community. The restaurant was situated on the only paved road in the village, right next to the bus depot. The rest of the community consisted of hard-packed dirt roads and buildings made of mud walls with thatched straw roofs. Water was drawn from wells, and only 10 percent of the households in the community had electricity. Chickens roamed freely from yard to yard, and families that were better off owned some pigs. Near the village were the tombs of two historical figures from Korea's past, a famous general and a king. There was also a famous Buddhist temple nearby that drew tourists from all over Korea.

Our restaurant was one of the few concrete buildings, and it had a sign that said "Ing Bin Low," Chinese for "A Very Important Person's Restaurant." When you entered the restaurant, the first thing you noticed was the fragrant aroma of steaming bowls of freshly cooked noodles with black bean sauce. For the patrons who had more money to spend, there was also sweet-and-sour beef with roasted wheat tea. At the back of the restaurant, my father would be standing over a huge wok, while my mother would be in the front greeting customers and serving them. My parents had come from Shandong Province in China, and the transition was not easy. They worked extra hard to make a living, which left only my grandmother to care for me.

Throughout my childhood, I was made to feel that I was cursed. After my mother gave birth to me, she became greatly ill. Every doctor she went to was unable to help her. She was introduced through one of her relatives to a shaman who told her that my spirit was too strong—it was slowly strangling my mother's spirit and would eventually consume the rest of my family. In an act of desperation, my mother had the shaman perform a ceremony on me to be spiritually adopted by another family, which required changing my name. I was too young to understand what was going on, but I couldn't help but feel unwanted and rejected. I felt something was wrong with me. Then one day when I was three, I was playing at a construction site while my grandmother watched over me. When she saw a truck backing up in my direction, she jumped in between me and the truck. She saved my life by sacrificing hers. After that incident, my family never let me forget that I was the cause of all their problems. Now that my grandmother was gone, I was passed around to the neighbors that were available to watch me. I felt lost seeing unfamiliar faces every day.

When I was old enough to go out and play with friends, I started to realize I was different from the other kids. Evenings were the peak time for my family's restaurant, so every night when my friends went home to their families, I usually fell asleep alone in the back room.

One morning later that spring, I went to meet my friends where we would normally play, but they never showed up. After several hours of waiting, I started walking back home past the neighborhood school and saw my friends on the other side of the fence. All of them had new matching clothes with yellow hats, name tags, and handkerchiefs. I wondered why I was not included. I thought I was being punished and was filled with confusion and fear. I thought I had lost my only companions. When I got home, my mom told me I would be joining them soon, and I was relieved.

The following week, my mom took me on a two-hour bus ride to Seoul, the capital of South Korea, and from there we got on a train for another two hours until we reached the end of the line at a port city called Inchon, where there was a large Chinese community. From the station my mom and I walked to a building nearby that I learned was a boardinghouse. It was a pre-war, two-story, Western-style red brick structure. Inside, its wooden floor and stairs creaked and groaned with every step. The air was stale and the walls were rough, made of the same red brick as the exterior. It was there that my mother dropped me off with a few words of instruction. I did not know where I was. My friends weren't there, and I didn't see any familiar faces except my second-oldest sister Lan and my brother Shung, who were both in their teens at the time. I was confused and terrified. I felt like I'd been dropped off in the middle of a dark, stormy ocean where I had no sense of direction and was constantly treading water while worrying about being swallowed by a big wave. I was scared that I would never see my friends or my parents again. I started to think that I should not have asked for so much.

This particular boardinghouse was for Chinese refugee kids whose families, like mine, did not live locally. There were kids of different ages ranging from 10 to 17, and being only 6 years old at the time, I was an exception. The first day of school, I saw my classmates accompanied by their families while I was sitting alone and wondering what I had done that was so wrong that my parents had given up on me. I was terrified by the fact that I could be all alone in the world.

At the boardinghouse, I was bullied and teased every day. I had to learn how to defend myself. I found myself getting into fights frequently. I treated every slight as a personal attack. I became bitter and angry even though I was able to visit my parents on the weekends. They were often too busy to hear about my problems, however, and I did not want to make the same mistake twice—the last time I had bothered them, I had been sent away.

Every morning a facilitator would corral all the kids into a dining hall, where we stood in a line to be issued a bowl of plain rice. We would then be seated at an assigned bench. It looked like a park picnic table, with five kids on each side. On each table there were two bowls of stew or stir-fried vegetables for ten children to share. I had to stretch as far as I could just to reach the food. On top of that, I was expected to finish my meal on time, along with the older kids. It felt like I was trapped in a lion's den, surrounded by predators. I felt hopeless. I was not allowed to be a kid anymore. I had to fight to survive.

In third grade, I was relocated to another school in Seoul, where the largest Chinese refugee community was located. My older siblings and I were renting a room. On the way back from school one day, I fell asleep on the bus and missed my stop. When I finally woke up, it was dark outside and I was the only one left. I was terrified. I felt desperate and sick to my stomach. All I could think about was how to survive. I pretended to be asleep until the bus reached its final destination. When the bus driver approached me, I told him that I had missed my stop and I didn't have any money. He was nice enough to let me stay on the bus until he headed back down the route again. I was relieved. But then I realized that I was cold and hungry. It was a long drive back. I found myself worrying about being yelled at by my sister, but when I finally arrived home, my siblings had not even noticed that I had been gone for the past six hours. This grotesque reality started to affect my beliefs. I felt I was alone in the world, lost and oblivious to what the world might bring.

During my second year of junior high school, I was a loner without any close friends. I always felt out of place. At this time my siblings had gone off to college, and I was living alone in a rental room and losing interest in school. This was when I met Li, who paid attention to me and showed me kindness. Her presence gave me a sense of comfort, and I felt that somehow she understood me. She was the first person since my grandmother who made me feel appreciated. I had finally made an emotional connection with another person. But I despaired because I knew inevitably I would be abandoned again. A few weeks later, my fears were realized when my family moved to the United States. I thought to myself, Is this my fault, am I being punished? I felt angry, but I feared the consequences of asking questions or complaining. Things started to seem hopeless, and I felt more inadequate than ever.

I was 14 years old when I immigrated with my family to a foreign land. My parents decided to settle in downtown Los Angeles, near Koreatown, in a two-bedroom apartment. It was a 1970s-style, three-story building with a small swimming pool in the front and an elevator with a glass wall that faced the front street. Living in the living room without privacy perpetuated my sense of uncertainty, like I was not there permanently. But the hardest part was being under the same roof with my parents. Growing up in a boardinghouse, I had never learned how to be a member of a family. Loving and being loved were foreign concepts to me. I had never had anyone to rely on before.

My first day at my new school was a disaster. I had enrolled in a junior high named John Burroughs. Like many Los Angeles schools, it had gang problems.

It was a racially diverse school with Whites, Blacks, Hispanics, and Koreans, and one other Chinese student besides me. I thought I had to prove myself constantly. That first day, I got into my first fight of many, solely because of the language barrier. I was emotionally immature, and I felt like my head was barely above water. In this new world where I couldn't even order a hamburger without help, I felt like I was drowning. While my parents thought I was in school, I would wander the streets aimlessly. One day when I was at the arcade, there were other Chinese kids there, and I found a connection with them instantly. They were members of a Chinese gang. At that time I did not understand the concept of a gang, nor did I care. I just wanted to belong. My desire to be loved, accepted, appreciated, and validated overshadowed my sense of right and wrong. I was willing to do anything to stay a part of the gang. In many ways it made me feel I had purpose.

Years of pent-up anger, rejection, and insecurity created and nurtured a monster that was unleashed through a destructive and violent lifestyle. It ultimately led me to make horrible life-changing decisions. My choices and lifestyle led to a prison sentence of life without the possibility of parole (LWOP), a slow death sentence. I arrived in prison with the same buried emotions I'd been carrying since childhood. Because of my distorted worldview, my conviction seemed outrageous to me. I established a pattern of finding fault with everyone else in the misguided belief that it would make me feel better.

During the early years of my incarceration, I felt completely lost. My life seemed meaningless. At first I pursued pleasure and power by getting high on anything that was available and involving myself in prison politics. I also sold drugs and preyed on the weak. Somehow I believed it would lessen the pain and fill the void in my heart, but it only left me feeling empty and worthless. I was a convicted criminal, a gang member, a drug addict—unlovable. I had to make a choice: I could continue with my current lifestyle and end up destroying my life, I could commit suicide to stop the pain, or I could get some help. I started to realize the seriousness of my situation. I needed a divine intervention.

Growing up, my mother was Buddhist, and our family observed all Buddhist traditions. Those memories taught me to believe that somehow pleading to Buddha would solve my problems and ease my pain. Therefore, I attended

Buddhist service to seek truth in divinity. During one service, I was told by a Buddhist monk that Buddha was not a god but a human teacher. I couldn't believe what I was hearing. It seemed like everything I had thought I'd known was wrong. What the monk said made me feel like I was free-falling into a bottomless pit. I was struggling to grab on to anything, even the air. In the midst of my confusion, I received a letter from a person named Angie. She belonged to the Valley Korean United Methodist Church, a prison ministry that visits and shares the Gospel with incarcerated Asians. It was one of very few letters I had received in my 16 years of incarceration. It was handwritten and personal, which gave it a warm feel. The content of the letter was the opposite of what I expected, as all they wanted was to get to know me and hear how I was doing. They made me feel welcomed and accepted, although I was skeptical of their motives. They offered to visit me, but I was not ready. I was still very protective of my emotions and I did not want to be disappointed again. I was cautious about the whole thing, but my overwhelming desire for acceptance slowly overcame the fear I had, and after a while I gave in.

The day they came to visit, I was nervous. As soon as I stepped into the visiting room, I noticed two Asian ladies standing in the middle, wandering around and scanning the room to the left and to the right with a suspicious expression on their faces, as if not knowing what to do or what to expect. They were waiting and searching for an Asian face to appear. After I checked in with an officer, I turned and faced them, and we made eye contact. They seemed relieved and surprised. We greeted each other in Korean. One was Angie, who had been writing me, and the other was her friend Joanne. We sat at our assigned table. I had a preconceived notion that it was going to be a long day talking about Jesus. To my surprise, however, it was all about me. They wanted to know how I was doing. It reminded me of being with Li, way back when I was 14 years old. It was comforting, and it made me feel secure, appreciated, and welcomed. They did not suffocate me with religion—instead, these total strangers made me feel loved. I started to wonder if this was the love people described as agape, or godly love. Out of gratitude, I started a correspondence Bible study. The more I learned about Christianity, the more I wanted to learn about God and this fellow named Jesus, a carpenter, and His rebirth. I learned that I might receive a brand-new life and identity if I called out His name and confessed my sins.

121

One day I received a Bible that was engraved with "Jesus Loves Kenny." Those three words made me feel worthy of being loved. It was like a magic spell. The words carried an undeniable power that gave me, in a gentle and inviting way, a strong desire to surrender myself.

It was Monday, March 17, 2014, around 11:00 p.m. I was locked in the cell as usual, staring at the TV screen mindlessly and stressing about life. All of a sudden I felt an urge to pray and reach out to God. But I didn't know how to start a prayer. Should it begin with "Heavenly Father"? Or "Father in Heaven"? Or should I introduce myself? I did not want to disrespect or piss off God. It was awkward not knowing how to start, so I just quietly said, "Jesus, are you there?" I called out His name and asked for His help. Immediately I was overcome by a warmth so powerful I lost control of my thoughts and emotions. I let down all the protective guards that I had carried all my life and had been hiding behind. The anguish of being neglected, abandoned, and rejected by everyone began pouring out of me. I confessed all my secrets and past sins, right down to the candy I stole as a child. In true repentance I found His mercy, forgiveness, and love. That night I cried myself to sleep. Since God saved me, my life has not been the same. I now have purpose and identity. My longing for acceptance and validation has been fulfilled by accepting Christ as my Lord and Savior.

Since finding my spiritual path in Christ, I have been able to face the truth. I need to accept responsibility. I realize that it was my choice to associate with gangs and that my participation was a contributing factor to everything that followed. I can no longer say that what has happened to me is anyone's fault but my own. When I was lost, I was blind to the truth.

Through Christ, I started to live truthfully. He empowered me to set aside my pride and to be humble. I began to understand how my low self-esteem and feelings of rejection had shaped me and led me to develop a defective character. Through that insightful revelation, I came to accept responsibility for the harms I had caused and to understand the fear and pain I had brought on my community and my family. As I took responsibility for all my past actions, I began to feel sincere remorse, and the most difficult thing was realizing I can never undo the harm I've caused. As a Christian living a life of repentance, a day does not pass without me feeling regret and remorse for all the victims of my past actions.

These days my spiritual path has provided me with a small opportunity to make amends through correspondence with the congregation of my church. I have been able to help our congregation's troubled immigrant youth and their families, to attempt to stop the cycle of gang culture. One such person I was able to help was a young man named David. He was an athletic 16-year-old on the high school football team who was getting average grades. One day he was asked to shoot someone to be initiated into a gang. Thank God that his father Bill reached out to me at an early stage, when I was able to share with David about my past and the consequences I am living with. Thankfully David was able to make the right decision and not join the gang. This experience taught me that my broken past could save someone's life. This is my divine purpose. Helping David profoundly changed my perception of myself and the world I live in. Since then, I have reached out to many other troubled youth. I truly believe these opportunities are a blessing from God.

As I sought God in my life, I developed a strong desire to serve Him, which led me to enroll at the Harvest Bible University, where I have been working toward a master of divinity degree. I have also earned two associate degrees through Coastline Community College, because I realized that educating myself would help me to be more effective when working with at-risk youth and my fellow incarcerated people. Instead of being the angry, insecure, and resentful person I once was, I am now more confident and empathetic with others. Because of what I've been through, I can better understand what others are experiencing. I can now honestly say I feel forgiven by God. Since finding Christ, I am at peace. I was lost and now I am found.

I was once a foreigner, a refugee, and a stranger to my family. I believed my existence was so insignificant that no one would ever care for me. I did not understand my own value. These days, I still carry those pains but don't dwell on them—rather, I keep them as a reminder of who I once was and use them as a motivation to continue my growth. I truly believe my past struggles and painful experiences have their purpose, because they have played a large part in making me who I am today. Most importantly, I have come to learn what true freedom looks like. As the late Nelson Mandela once said, "For to be free is not merely to cast off one's chains, but to live in a way that respects and enhances the freedom of others." I think Mr. Mandela perfectly summarized the meaning of true freedom.

I continually set goals and strive to achieve them. My current short-term goals are to complete my master of divinity degree, finish an Offender Mentor Certification Program (OMCP), and become a drug and alcohol counselor. My long-term goal is to serve God through humanity. My transformation has only been possible through God's mercy, His Grace, and His Love. It is a love that has no boundaries of race, ethnicity, or status. A love that forgives. No matter how great the sin is, God's love is greater. This love has given me a brand-new life.

Thou Shall Not Judge

Ricky May

society hates to be judged
but we're the ones quick to judge a book by its cover
whether a convicted felon, a prostitute,
or a struggling mother, drug addict or plain Jane being abused
whatever the label we choose
superficial don't you say?
most turn a blind eye to their neighbor
accepting that they suffer in silence
fearful to intervene
far from understanding it could have changed the course of their life

still we choose to stand by

WHAT IF, I ask myself every day of my life
WHAT IF, I would have spoken my fears
WHAT IF, I had the courage and strength
WHAT IF, I took the risk

the screams inside are so deafening
the scares and emotion so vivid
the pain and suffering so revealing
still society chooses to stand by and judge me
aren't we all responsible?
never should you stand by
when you see thy neighbor struggling
I starve, not from hunger
but from the lack of a helping hand from my fellow man

because of what society has beaten into me
harsh words of rejection, at times physical abuse
my mind plays tricks on me
there's more to my life than the naked eye
behind these walls I've built

Unveiling the Curtains
Tien N. Nguyen

It's been a long day and here I am playing cops and robbers with my brothers and cousins. As the bright sun goes to sleep and darkness approaches, we all run inside the house. It's crowded inside with adults conversing loudly and karaoke music blaring in the background. All the kids know how to go into the room without being seen. I take off my shoes and make my way through the litter of shoes on the floor. I walk past my father and hear him call out, "Meo[18], come here!" With excitement and joy I go to my father. I have never sat with the grown-ups before. I sit on my father's lap, and he tells me to open my mouth. At that moment I could not be any happier. I comply with his demand as he picks up a shot glass and begins pouring liquid into my mouth. With great disgust I begin to spit it out and cough. A rise of laughter explodes in the room as I struggle to comprehend what is happening. I glance at my father, and all I see is disappointment and contempt written on his face. My stomach drops as my chest tightens up. It hurts me to see that expression on his face because all I want is his love and approval. His anger is fire to my ears as it burns up any hopes of me pleasing him. I walk away with my head held low in shame and guilt. That night, I tell myself the next opportunity that presents itself to please my father, I will do what he wants without betraying any dissatisfaction.

Over the next few weeks, opportunities present themselves again and again. Each time I go to where the adults are and pick up a shot glass and drink it without making a face. My father smiles and pats me on the head. In those moments I feel valued and loved. I even brag about it to my brothers and cousins, until one day my mother sees me drinking from a shot glass and scolds and beats me. My father does not come to my aid; instead he laughs like everyone else. Overwhelmed with shame, humiliation, and confusion, I do not understand what I have done wrong, I do not know how to please both my

---

18 Meo: Means cat in Vietnamese, a term of endearment

parents, who are giving me mixed messages. One thing is certain, however—there are things I can do with my father that I should keep secret from my mother.

My childhood continued on like this for some time. The traumas I experienced were exacerbated by the constant moving to different homes and new schools. Almost every year I was the new kid at school, forced to let go of friends as soon as I made them, which left me feeling unstable and disoriented. I was surrounded by people, yet on the inside I felt so lonely. Those good-byes hurt me deeply every time and left me questioning, "Why?" I blamed my pain on my parents and viewed them as the sole cause of my suffering. This pain was compounded by the physical and emotional abuse I experienced at home. I felt there was no safe haven in my life, nowhere I truly belonged.

My parents disciplined me with a broomstick, and the more I cried, the more punishment I received. This helped reaffirm my belief that expressing my emotions was dangerous. When I spoke my mind to my parents, the result was a quick slap to my face. Yes, the physical abuse I experienced was painful, but the real scars existed in the emotional realm. During my elementary school years I asked my parents to attend school events such as talent shows, science fairs, parent-teacher conferences, and graduations. Every time the response was "Why would we go?" or "What for?" or "We don't have time for that." Those words cut me deeper than any physical pain could have. It instilled insecurity and a negative image of myself. I wondered what was wrong with me. I attended those events alone, watching other kids laugh and smile with their parents as I sat with loneliness overwhelming my senses. Often I asked myself, "Why couldn't I have had different parents?" or "Why are my parents not like theirs?" After elementary school I stopped asking those questions that only gave me a sense of painful rejection.

The year is 1998, and I am nine years old. At this point in my life, I am about to experience a most terrifying event. The day begins as usual, but as the sun sets I hear my parents arguing on the other side of the door. Curious about the insidious uproar, my brothers and I open the door to see what is going on. I hear my father accuse my mother of cheating and wanting to leave him. She responds by agreeing that she is leaving him. Those few words put me in a state of shock. As their quarrel continues, the fury in my father's eyes burns brighter. My mother sits there firm in her stance. I have seen them argue before, but never like this. I can barely make sense of their words as the fear inside me grows. My father suddenly darts to the kitchen drawer and pulls out a knife. Time slows down as I watch my father lunge toward my mother like a hungry predator. My mother reaches for his arm to stop him as my father spews out evil words through clenched teeth. Struck with terror, I am frozen in my tracks.

My entire life is shattered in that moment. I want to help my mother and plead for my father to stop. Yet my legs will not move, and no words escape my lips. As I stand there petrified, my older brother rushes to my mother's aid, grabbing my father's arm and begging him to stop. My brother has done what I want to do. But I am too afraid. My brother is a hero to me. This chaotic scenery plays out before me through a veil of watery curtains. My legs finally move, but in the opposite direction, as I retreat into a nearby closet. I sit there crying into my lap, hoping that all this is simply a nightmare. I tell myself that I am a coward and that I should have helped. The fear anchors me down and paralyzes all my motor functions. In time I fall asleep, and when I wake up the nightmare seems to have ended.

The next day no one speaks of what happened the night before. I watch my father pack his things and walk right out the door, never saying a word. There is a sense of relief, confusion, and sadness. All I hear from my mother is that my no-good father is leaving me and that he isn't coming back.

In the following years my family moved twice and I was left wondering which man my mother was dating would become my stepfather. I watched as my mother had relationships with multiple men and noticed how each one tried to bribe me for my acceptance. I felt the power I wielded manipulating them and complying with their requests. I was rewarded with money, gifts, and most importantly, a sense of value. My small world consisted of only a handful of people—my two brothers, my mother, and her boyfriends. This small world grew when I moved to San Lorenzo.

I remember that first day at Bohannon Middle School like any other day—I had been the new kid so many times that the fear was familiar. It definitely wasn't my first time feeling awkward and shy. A year went by and I started to feel stable in this new home. For once in my life, I would stay in the same place for more than four years. It was in this town that I would make lifelong friends and forge connections with others in a way I never had before. It was here that I took the reins of my life. I spent more time with my friends than anyone else. With them, I felt loved and valued. I felt like I belonged. The time I spent with my friends was an escape from what was going on in my family. I was embarrassed to bring my friends over because on the occasions that I did, my mother would be right there giving us the death stare. My friends feared my mother, but they never knew the fear and pain I kept deep inside. I was scared to let them know. I was scared to lose them. I was scared to be vulnerable. Underneath it all, I did not want to feel the loneliness I had felt before. I chose to wear a mask that was visible only to me. No one else knew when it was on, or off.

The life I chose to live was a mystery to many. For I was living a double life. One moment I was the morally upright person, displaying all the positive characteristics my role models had taught me. People around me admired and adored me for my positive acts. On paper, I excelled in academics, and it would seem that my parents' dream for me was coming true. What my parents were unaware of was my darker side. A more rebellious side that was only compliant in order to get what I wanted. Because of the lack of communication between us, my mother could never tell what was on my mind, and she never bothered to ask. Her focus was on the grades I brought home. But I used my grades as a tool to escape from my mother's ridicule. Only those closest to me saw glimpses of this darker being.

My right hand seems to be possessed by an unknown entity as I try to write the next few lines. There is a voice inside me that tells me to stop. A most sinister voice that wants to prevent me from healing and accepting the truth. I struggle to continue writing about the birth of such darkness. There is a clear connection between my traumas and the choices I made. The inner demon deep in my internal inferno cries out in pain every time I express my emotions. The two sides of me that have been battling for years lead to constant conflict in my values, goals, and beliefs. I stop writing and sit in meditation. With eyes closed, I watch as thoughts and feelings arise and fade away. A light of clarity shines through my mind as the demon inside me reveals its true form.

There is a young boy no older than nine years old cowering in a closet. As I approach the boy, the closer I get, the more I notice an aura of anger, fear, and pain emanating from him in this empty space. Standing before the boy, him glaring at me like a hungry wolf, I kneel down to meet his gaze. I see all the struggles he's been through in those eyes, all the pain. This poor child has been with me for decades, and in moments of stress he lashes out at the world. Words flow from my mouth as I whisper, "What happened in your life was not okay, but you're going to make it, and know that I love you." With open arms I embrace the pain-ridden child with compassion. I hear his soft cries and feel warm tears on my shoulder. All that hostile aura dissipates in an instant. My consciousness returns to the present moment, and I notice the tears flowing as my entire being radiates with peace. With a most invigorating life energy, the words from my pen begin to flow again.

In high school I did anything to gain my friends' acceptance and love. At times it came at the expense of hurting others, whether it was physical fights that I always justified or hurtful words that I inflicted upon others. All I was concerned with was how I could get everyone to notice me. My academics were satisfactory, and so I gave myself permission to act out. I manipulated people to do what I wanted, and I used violence as a way to show my friends I would do anything for them. In my mind I was the protector, and not that cowardly kid hiding in the closet. I told myself this was my time to be the hero. Over time my aggressive behavior became a habit, and I became a bully. My aggression gave me the control I had always desired, so I latched on to it as a primary tool to assert myself in uncomfortable situations. I had become what I believed I hated the most. Drunk with power and delusion, I had little rationality left in me. My ego was inflated by the praise and affection others gave me. Unable to contain my ego, I allowed it to run rampant. Leaving a path of pain and suffering in my wake.

In 2007, I left home to go to college and lived in a house filled with friends. I was genuinely happy at this time in my life. I used every celebratory event as an excuse to drink and go wild. It got to the point where drinking became the norm. My problem was that I wanted to stand out in everything I did. So I chose to drink the most and be the loudest one in the room. I believed that this would give me the acknowledgment and recognition I desired, and it did. Yes, even at this later age, the child of years ago was still making decisions.

I continued to harm those around me with little or no awareness of their feelings. Alcohol gave me the confidence I lacked. It was another tool I used to gain what I desired. Alcohol and my aggression went hand in hand. It was easy to blame my belligerent acts on the booze. While in college I was involved in several fights. Fights I thought were justified because I was only protecting my friends. My view became even more distorted when I was drunk. I perceived threats where there were none.

In 2009, my little cousin was beaten to death at a party that I had refused to attend with him. I had told him I had to work early in the morning. Before college our relationship was as tight as brothers, but it deteriorated over time due to my actions and lack of communication. For years I had been avoiding him because of my own guilt and shame. Now I blamed myself for what had happened to him and constantly had thoughts of "what if." The pain, guilt, and shame surrounded my life. I had not been there in his time of need. What was more disheartening was that I had never been able to say how much I loved him and how sorry I was. I was a coward, just like so many years ago. My unwillingness to be vulnerable left me in greater pain. I hated this feeling and dove deeper into my addiction. I spoke little about my cousin and did not want to be with his family. I felt immense shame and guilt around them. The more I used substances, the less I felt these unpleasant feelings. I could not picture enjoying life as much as I did without substances. My addiction was at an all-time high for me after graduating college. My success in life was once again a justification for my behaviors. Behaviors that would lead to a lifetime of suffering for so many people, and ultimately a tragic loss of life.

December 20, 2012, was a day for celebration and joy. My girlfriend and friends were graduating. We all lived under one roof. The 12 of us were preparing for a celebratory day. I woke up that morning with excitement and anticipation. That day I was also going to meet my girlfriend's parents again. To deal with my anxiety, I took a Xanax pill and watered it down with a couple of beers. Filled with a false sense of confidence and bravado, I put on a mask that I believed would impress her parents. Yet it only seemed to draw them further away from acknowledging me the way I desired.

As the day progressed, I drank more and more. I had gone from partying at home to going downtown barhopping. At the after-party, things got out of control. My friend and a fellow partygoer got into an argument and were separated. In this moment I was triggered to do what I had done before to protect my friends, or at least that's what I told myself. All the day's earlier moments of dissatisfaction and the emotions that I had been running away from since childhood were alive in me now. Not wanting to feel such unpleasantness, I chose to take control of the situation with violence. Being inebriated only helped to fuel the anger that was boiling with moral judgment. My mind concocted a threat, as hostile thoughts ran rampant. Compelled by those thoughts and a brew of unpleasant emotions, I took it upon myself to physically assault two people and murder another.

Suddenly, the pen in my hand stops. My mind starts recalibrating and evaluating all the suffering I have created. I ask myself, "How many more must continue to suffer because of my selfish and impulsive decisions?" My body and its entire existence trembles as remorse washes over me. I recall the sorrows during my trial. All the pain that was expressed before my very eyes and ears. I close my eyes to sit with all the suffering. An endless stream of water flows as I drown myself in the pain of those I have harmed.

A mother who lost her son cries out in pain. The sound of her voice still vibrates within me as I sit here. One by one, those I've harmed take center stage to express their pain. In that moment I see myself with my head down, filled with guilt and shame. I can still hear the words of those who were harmed as their sorrow and pain lingers in my mind. A pain so great it drags me to the pits of hell. I rely on my practice to stay centered, as I cultivate what is alive in me and connect to the needs of those I have harmed. With a deep intake of breath, I feel the cold air enter the nostril gates as I take in all the suffering. A long extended exhale follows as compassion radiates for all those whom I have harmed, including myself. This is part of the healing process for me, and although it causes a tremendous amount of distress, it is a process I need.

As I finish writing my story, I feel completely depleted. A sense of relief is draped over my shoulders as they relax. After all the reluctance and fear of writing about my childhood and the harm I've caused others, I find peace. I feel an openness and strength in being vulnerable. The guilt and shame I felt about dishonoring my family by writing is exiled. I am finally letting go of all the suffering I held inside, and I have come to a peaceful acceptance of my past. I see now how the events in my past connect with the strategies I chose in life to meet my needs. All of my pain is in those sheets of paper.

Who would have thought I would find the support I needed within these prison walls? In 2015, I was convicted of second-degree murder. At that moment I thought I had lost everything and would spend the rest of my life in prison. The feeling of hopelessness was persistent. To banish such feelings I changed my distorted thinking and sought help from others. Looking back, prison has helped me change into a better person.

My name is Tien Nguyen. I am of Vietnamese descent, and I was born November 22, 1989, in Mesa, Arizona. I am currently 31 years old. I've spent the majority of my life living in the Bay Area in California. I graduated from San Jose State University with a degree in industrial technology. At the age of 23, I committed the horrendous act of murder and was sentenced to 16 years to life. Today, I am working as an alcohol and drug counselor with the prison population, invoking change from within for those with a checkered past. My dream of a world where people can make connections with one another through empathy and compassion keeps me motivated to share what has been illuminated for me. I am a son, a brother, a friend, and so much more, but remove all those labels and I am simply a human being, just like you.

Lost Dream / "Path of Hope"
Chandra Kishor

Truth is golden
Internalized with serenity
Eyes open as smiling flowers
Green green flowing fields
Waving under blue blue skies
Life is priceless,
As Eden precision
Home by Lake Tranquil
Health pearl precious
By tall tall trees
Clear blue sky clouds dancing
By green green grass
Valley of small hills
Touch of tenderness
By Apsara Angelic
Sheer electric madness
Enlightened dreamings
Sensuating forged reality
Heavens of knowledge showering
Ever falling for seeking
To keep to share this treasure
Is wealth as emeralds and rubies
Gleaming personas sparkling
Joys of life are strength n' wealth.

To strive n' smile
Love & Gods deserted

Running miles for love we cherish
To sing & dance, knives in back
Crimson clover hearts - emotions
Making friends smile for miles
While fear n' worry hounding
As lions n' tigers wolves creeping
In stealth as pearls of wisdom
Pure in mind is health n' wealth
Shinier granite as snowy diamonds
Amber jasper pearl precious -
Proprietors offer as treasures
Hope of Path - lost as jewel journey
Priceless precision proper
Prescription for/of Prosperity.

The Chronicles of Hung T. Ly
Hung T. Ly

Friday, March 24, 2006, Sacramento County Superior Court: "It is the decision of this court to order that Hung T. Ly be committed to state prison for the penalty prescribed by law, life without the possibility of parole. Further…it is the decision of this court to order a consecutive indeterminate term of 25 years to life," the judge said. "You do have the right to appeal this sentence. Do you understand?" I replied, "Yes, Your Honor."

The slam of the gavel punctuated the sentence, and it hit me like a slap to the face as I heard a woman crying behind me. I couldn't see who she was and I acted like I didn't care, but despair was my true feeling. That was the worst news I had ever received in my 21 years of existence.

Life without the possibility of parole, commonly known as "LWOP." A sentence to serve with the remainder of my natural life. And when my spirit thinks it's time to move on, it's held back to serve 25 years to life. No redemption. No second chance.

•••

I was born in the summer of 1984, and I was raised by a single mother and half siblings in South Sacramento, California. Four years before I was born, our family immigrated to the United States of America from Vietnam, by way of a Hong Kong refugee camp. Although we come from Vietnam, we are ethnically Chinese. In the United States, integrating into a new society was difficult due to the cultural and language barriers between our family, other immigrants, and Americans…

My first home was a poverty-level apartment complex. Mom did her best to raise three children on her own—while working numerous jobs, attending adult school, and learning the culture of a foreign land. We didn't have much, but we were sustained with assistance from relatives, food banks, and welfare. As a first-generation Chinese American, I was one of the first in my family to reap the benefits from the Land of the Free and the Land of Opportunity. And I was one of the first to carry all the hopes and dreams my family had for me to live a successful, healthy life in a new country.

We moved into Section 8 housing when I was about three years old. Family time was interrupted shortly thereafter when a big man suddenly jumped into our backyard and ran into our home. He entered through the open sliding glass door and advanced toward Mom, where he proceeded to pull on her arm—an attempted kidnapping. Shocked and confused, I stood helplessly watching as Sis yelled, "I'm calling 911!" The intruder unlocked our front door in a panic and fled, leaving the door wide open. He ran across the street and was promptly apprehended in the parking lot of a church.

I remember listening to Mom recall a time, before my birth, about an encounter with racism. While walking to school, she and two aunts were called names and attacked by Americans. They didn't understand what was said but knew it wasn't anything good. Hearing that story made me feel uncomfortable because I faced similar treatment from schoolmates. The kids were relentless in making me feel rejected and inferior because of my race. "Open your eyes!" and "Go back to where you came from!" were some of the things they yelled. Startled, I usually respond with "F@#% you, I was born here!"

Big Bro was going in and out of jail at the time. He spent time in juvenile hall and the Boys Ranch, a boot camp for troubled youth located on the east side of Sacramento County. When he was home, he would receive regular visits from probation officers and many friends. He and his friends traveled in American or Japanese rides with custom paint and wheels and subwoofers in the trunk. They wore Nike basketball shoes, Starter sports-team jackets, and gold jewelry. They had girlfriends; it seemed like they did what they wanted to do, which captured my attention. I couldn't wait to grow up so that I could do the same.

One evening, members of the Sacramento Police Department's gang task force kicked their way into Big Bro's bedroom with guns drawn, but the room was empty. Visibly upset, Mom yelled in Cantonese at one of the officers who was Chinese that they were going to pay for the broken door. The raid frightened me, and I believed the authorities were there to hurt him or take him away from us. From then on, I disliked and distrusted law enforcement, especially Asian cops, who I felt were sellouts.

I soon learned that my brother's lifestyle came with other consequences besides cars and clothes and girls, but that knowledge didn't deter me. At about the age of nine, my life was put in jeopardy when rival gang members committed two drive-bys on our home. I survived the shootings—physically sound, but mentally disturbed. I felt insecure living in my own home. I was hypervigilant. Whenever a car approached our neighborhood, I would cautiously peek out the blinds to see who it was.

The shootings went on and on, and I can recall Big Bro returning with his car riddled with gunfire. Unfortunately, the gangsters achieved their goal when they hit their intended target, critically wounding him. I was devastated when Sis informed us of the incident, and I thought that I was going to lose a family member to gang violence. From what I heard, he was ambushed while hanging out by the front entrance of a local pool hall. Fortunately, he recovered, but the scars on his torso serve as a reminder of his past gang lifestyle.

Experiencing these traumatic events impacted my underdeveloped mind, infecting me with anger and resentment. Oftentimes, I would promise myself that when I got older and found out who the shooters were, I would kill them. With an irrational and dysfunctional thought process, I believed the world was unfair and that the only way to succeed in life was to utilize violence to solve conflicts and to have the upper hand. To defend myself and my family, I armed myself with anything capable of inflicting harm. At age 11, I started carrying pocketknives and kept a Louisville Slugger in my room in case of another intruder, or for any other reason. I was on guard and ready to attack.

By the time I was 12 and in the sixth grade, I thought I was grown and independent. My paternal father attempted to come into my life for several years, but I rejected him. I felt that I had gone through childhood without him, so I didn't need him. I got into fights and began hanging out with troubled peers. We smoked Marlboro Lights, drank beer and wine, and carved gang epithets on school doors with pocketknives.

In high school, I was aligned with a big crowd of Asians, and with them, I felt empowered and accepted. To preserve my position, I conformed to the group culture by promoting hate, intimidation, and violence. I found it difficult to learn, and the temptation to skip class to hang out with friends left me with straight F's and truancies. When I returned on the first day of what I thought was my junior year, I discovered I had been dropped from the roster. That was when I decided that school was not meant for someone like me. I was a high school dropout without a job—a bad combination. At that time, the only thing I knew how to do to get spending money was to sell twamp sacs, baggies of marijuana the size of a quarter, to my peers. I even broke into cars to steal valuables. An easy way to get rich and I wasn't hurting anybody, or so I thought.

For the last two years of my freedom, I was out of control and disregarded the safety and feelings of everyone around me. I had a surplus of resentment from nearly two decades of on-the-edge existence. I spent most of that time hanging out and causing havoc in my community—from crashing parties to being involved in gang fights to harassing civilians.

I wanted to be feared and I demanded respect—and if I didn't receive it, I was willing to commit violence. Having no idea how to deal with the pain in my life, I hurt others in order to feel good about myself. "Crazy Hung" was what my friends called me, and I was doing everything in my means to live up to that adjective. Concerned with being associated with my crimes, I assumed the moniker "C-Ready," or simply, "C." A make-believe character who was determined to be the hardest gangster in town. In the end, I created many victims with that negative and hateful attitude.

•••

In the morning hours of January 10, 2004, I received a phone call on the landline from the police department, ordering me to gather my family and

140

to surrender outside. Peeking through the blinds, I saw the SWAT team van parked in front of our driveway with numerous masked men in full gear with guns drawn. Fearing for my family's safety, I quickly woke my siblings and notified my mom and stepdad of their instructions. We emerged from our home with hands in the air, and they took me into custody.

It was my first arrest, and as if I wasn't feeling hopeless enough, a deputy sheriff emphasized the "NO BAIL" listed on my booking receipt by circling it. That moment was a reality check. I understood then that I had recklessly thrown my life away, and that I would not see freedom again in this lifetime. I was 19 years old. While my peers graduated into college, I graduated into jail.

At my arraignment, I plead not guilty. My family initially retained a private attorney on my behalf, and I spent about a year and a half at the county jail, awaiting a jury trial. The deputy district attorney elected not to seek the death penalty. In July 2005, I was tried before a jury. Hoping that I would be exonerated of the charges filed against me, my state-appointed attorney argued my innocence.

I was shipped to the California Substance Abuse Treatment Facility in Corcoran soon after my conviction. At the classification hearing I was advised by the committee that due to the LWOP term, I was restricted to level 4 maximum security despite good behavior. "If I'm never returning to society or going to a safer facility," I thought, "what's the point of rehabilitation?" Needless to say, I felt discouraged.

At the prison, there wasn't much to do but hang out, exercise, attend school, or work. Violent incidents—race riots, staff assaults, fights, and stabbings—regularly occurred. They were followed by monthlong lockdowns that suspended visits and recreational activities. Designated as a "critical worker," I was allowed outside my cell. By working full-time and remaining in good behavior, my custody-level placement points decreased yearly, but I was left behind while non-LWOP prisoners were transferred to level 3 facilities.

During 2007 and 2008, a state-appointed attorney filed writs on my behalf to overturn my conviction. The California attorney general at the time, Jerry Brown, recommended that the state appellate court affirm my conviction, and the court agreed. The California Supreme Court denied review of my case thereafter. I was no longer afforded an attorney since the appeal was finalized, but I refused to give up. I turned to "jailhouse lawyers," who advised me that submitting new grounds to the trial court would pause the one-year time limit for filing a writ with the federal court. Based on this misleading information, I filed after the deadline and was denied solely for my untimeliness. Devastation ensued, and I was angry at myself for not doing my best to understand the law to fight for my life.

Initially, I felt like I didn't deserve that much time and continued to blame others for my circumstances—oblivious to the fact that I was the one who had created my misfortunes. I knew deep down in my heart that I was wrong, yet I couldn't accept responsibility for my crime. I didn't want to spend the rest of my life incarcerated. I was determined to make better choices and hung on to the hope that I would be free again someday.

At the beginning of 2013, the California Department of Corrections and Rehabilitation (CDCR) amended a regulation affecting thousands of LWOP prisoners in its custody. The act authorized those with low points to transfer to level 3 facilities throughout the state. Four months later, I arrived at California State Prison Solano in Vacaville.

At level 3 medium security, I noticed the presence of positive-minded men and the many programs and privileges the prison had to offer, which motivated me to start attending self-help groups. I received regular visits from family, and with the constant presence and support from loved ones, doing time was easier. We received Sacramento broadcasts, so I was able to see the place I once called home on the local news. I felt comfortable, and I didn't mind the idea of doing the rest of my life there.

After 3½ years of attending rehabilitative programs, I was summoned to my counselor's office for my annual program review. He advised me that since CDCR had authorized further reduction of security levels for LWOP prisoners, he would be recommending me to the classification committee for level 2 transfer. Within a couple of days, I moved to another facility at the prison. After 13 years caged in a two-man cell, I sat on the top bunk in a dorm setting drafting my story.

During my rehabilitation, California changed laws pertaining to LWOP sentences that allowed those who had committed their crimes before the age of 18 the ability to petition the court for a reduced sentence or receive a parole hearing in their 25th year of incarceration. Another LWOP bill allowed those who were convicted as an aider or abettor to petition for resentencing. I was excluded since I had been 19 at the time of my crime and a major participant in the offense.

Unwilling to accept my defeat, my relentless attitude pushed me to submit an application for commutation of sentence to the governor's office seeking clemency. With the application, I included certificates, laudatory reports from prison staff, written documents, and support letters from family and friends. Within eight months I was interviewed by a Board of Parole Hearings (BPH) investigator, who reported back to the governor's office. Then, in November 2018, one day before Thanksgiving, I was deemed worthy of a second chance when then California governor Jerry Brown—the same official who had previously opposed my appeal—reduced my sentence to a total of twenty years to life. The governor's act of clemency afforded me a parole consideration hearing, which had been denied to me in the past.

On November 10, 2020, I appeared before BPH commissioners through a videoconference. I took the opportunity at the hearing to express remorse by accepting full responsibility for the crime and admitting that my self-defense claim at the time of my arrest wasn't true. I spoke about my transformation, relapse prevention strategies, and parole plans. My endless hours of sitting in groups and doing the challenging work while serving the LWOP term was commended. The commissioners took everything into consideration and found me suitable for parole.

Finally, I paroled in spring 2021, when the world was in the early stages of recovering from the COVID-19 pandemic. I emerged from the other side of the secured perimeter of concrete wall, razor wire, and electric fence to the embrace of loved ones who never gave up on me. My two younger brothers are now adults, along with my six nieces and nephews. I'm happy to reunite with everyone.

It was 17 years earlier that my right to freedom as a US-born citizen was stripped away, and 15 years earlier that the judgment was handed down to lock me up for eternity. I'm extremely grateful for the mercy given to me and am excited to begin my new life as a responsible adult for the first time. It's now my lifelong duty to contribute to society and assist my fellow human beings in times of need. I'll do so in honor of the lives I've impacted by my past harmful behavior.

The journey of redemption continues...

Circles
John Lam

As a formerly incarcerated person who was sentenced to 26 years to life for a crime I committed at the age of 17, I often remember spending lonely holidays in a cell with nothing to look forward to other than a better meal during chow.

The better food we could expect depended on the holiday. We could get hot dogs, hamburgers, ice cream, and maybe a slice of watermelon on the Fourth of July. Turkey and all the canned fixings like pumpkin pie, cranberry sauce, and some mystery gravy on Thanksgiving. Then on Christmas, roast beef, wilted lettuce, and a small dinner roll—and at San Quentin we had something truly special, as over thirty community members would come in as Christmas carolers to serenade the whole building with live music. You could see all the guys on multiple tiers crowd over the railings with excited looks, some singing along, some giving whoops and whistles to cheer on the carolers. For a brief moment, we could forget we were alone.

As much as I tried to ignore the holidays by mentally calling it "just another day" or by putting a positive spin on it to ignore the pain of missing my family, those days were tough. They were yet another agonizing reminder of what had led me to prison and the distance between me and the free world.

I would often make deals with God on holidays, promising I would live my life the best way possible and make the best of every opportunity if God would only give me another chance to live free again.

Somewhere along the way, as the years went by, I stopped looking at holidays as days of agony or dealmaking. Instead I learned to use them as a time to reflect on the things I was most grateful for—simple things like good health, a loving family, a connection with God, and above all, a hope for a better future. This shift in my thinking led me to use holidays to write apology letters to my victims. As each successive year went by, I noticed that the letters got longer and longer as I discovered new things I had deprived my victims of that I hadn't realized the year before.

These writing exercises showed me how pain can last and develop. They gave me insight, because as I grew and my dreams changed, I could imagine what my victims might have wished for in their lives as well.

Perhaps the dealmaking with God worked after all. I learned how to change the holidays during my incarceration from days of agony to days of celebration, remembrance, and reflection.

And I must say that the letters of remorse played a key role in my thinking process and ultimately contributed to my early prison release.

Holidays hold a special significance for me. It was on a Christmas morning that I committed my life crime, and on Thanksgiving Day many years later, I received a miracle in the form of a governor's commutation. Exactly one year after my sentence was commuted, I was home in Los Angeles for Thanksgiving with my family of 17, including parents, siblings, in-laws, nieces, and nephews who had all driven down from Sacramento to be with me.

One of the things I wanted to do to show gratitude for the first holiday being with my family was to participate in a turkey giveaway. My brother-in-law, who happened to help organize a turkey giveaway in his community, gave me the opportunity to interact with community members and practice my Spanish as well. Volunteering during Thanksgiving allowed me to not just spend the holidays with my own family, but to also help ensure other families had an enjoyable family feast as well.

Holidays in the free world are truly something special to behold. To be with family, in celebration of good health, good food, and good company, is a real blessing. As I look back on my 16 years of incarceration, my fondest hope for my incarcerated brothers and sisters is that they keep the faith and hope alive.

Keep making deals with God, and see holidays as an opportunity to explore and reflect on gratitude and your impact on those you have harmed. For truly, God will reward your efforts with a clear mind, insight, and freedom.

When We Fight, We Win:
An Interview With Kanley Souet-Pich

Can you tell us a little bit about yourself, what you do, how you got into the organizing work with APSC, CERI, and ALC?

I'm an outreach worker, interpreter, and case manager at CERI. How I came on board with the organizing was through my husband being at-risk of being deported last year, 2019. I tried to be involved with every activity or every event that was being hosted by APSC, and I saw that you guys never gave up. It was just something I also wanted to do and I wanna be part of. I went to every event that I can, I tried to help with whatever I could. I'm not a good speaker, but I just wanted to be involved and help out. And I like to see people come home. You guys did help bring my husband and my cousin home in 2019 and 2020.

What was it like to be part of a deportation defense campaign?

I don't know if you [the interviewer] remember the day that you, Sarah, and Rhummanee were at CERI. We were talking about a two-minute storytelling thing for me and the elders, like how to tell your story in two minutes. I just really learned a breakdown of those two minutes! So I'm putting it together.

How was it like? It was nerve wracking! Like, *Dang, smart people. What are they doing? I wanna be like them, they're cool.* I ain't never seen no Cambodians come together for a good thing - it's always a bad thing, like tryna go jump somebody. I've never seen a bunch of Cambodians come together and fight for their freedom - for anybody's freedom. It's always the negative stuff we fight for.

And you mention your husband. What did he think of being a posterboy of a campaign? From your perspective, how did your kids react and participate? How did your relatives and other Khmer

elders feel during the campaign? Were they inspired to join the campaign?

Honestly, my husband did *not* want to do anything. I had to force him, I had to yell at him, I had to beat it in him: If we don't do it, you're not gonna come back! You have to allow us to do whatever they ask us to do. He still felt weird, but he did it. He was like, "Whatever, just sign it! Just do it." My family, they all did support us. They went to some of those things but they didn't stand out with me or speak with me. Honesty, I was very scared to even approach the CERI elders with this, 'cause I thought they were going to be judgemental about it–"[These people are always up to no good, now they're asking for people to help]"– I've had some negative things said to me before when I was doing that back then.

Do you think that the elders changed their mind being part of this campaign? Did you see a different side of them?

Yeah. They love me now! I'm like the person they run to now. Now they're even open to telling us stories about their children. Before this event, they don't really talk about their own children getting into trouble and needing help with those type of things. And now, I heard that they're opening up. I wasn't there before, but I heard that they never opened up, and now they're starting to because of what we went through, they're coming to tell me about it. Like, Can I help with this? Can I help with that?

How did your kids react and participate?

They always wanna go! The only place they didn't like to go was that long bus ride. But everywhere else, they loved going. They couldn't wait 'til Tuesday night to go to CERI. They had fun at the downtown city hall stuff. They were always happy to go. They would get mad when I don't tell them too. Certain days I called in for work and I went without them to some things. I forgot what it was, but they got mad at me.

They worked on their own speeches for some of the events. They also helped write support letters to the other people that was incarcerated. Even after my husband and cousin were released, they still loved going to rallies and holding signs. That one rally in San Francisco, the car one? They was hanging out at the top of the truck with a sign. I think that they enjoy it. Maragot was kind of shy but she's a lot better than me. She will go out there and speak.

Would you say this moment made them into little organizers now?

I think they can do anything now.

In what ways did this defense campaign impact you?

I didn't work until two years prior to the deportation case. I never thought about going back to school. I'm just gonna work and drive this bus wherever. I guess being around you guys and seeing how there's young Khmer educated people out here being leaders, my old self - why am I just letting my life go? I need to go back to school. And since then, I've been feeling good about myself. My English got better, my Cambodian got better. I'm more focused on school, and I have a lot of support from CERI with school too. I don't have time to hang out with friends anymore, you know, 'cause I'm not really getting wasted all the time anymore. I like it. I mean, my friends don't hate me because of it. They're all proud of me too.

I used to work at 3 in the morning. Now I can sleep 'til 9! Just kidding. I used to go to CERI nodding off though. The time when we were going for family therapy? I was nodding off because it was 4 in the afternoon, and I would wake up at 2 in the morning. I get more sleep now.

How has the campaign impacted your perspective on family, organizing, and the Khmer community, and hope? What gave you the strength to keep on fighting during this defense campaign?

I hear cases that you guys are fighting, but I didn't hear someone stopping the deportation. Or maybe there was, but I didn't know about it. I was kind of scared that it wasn't going to happen. But I kept going because Ny is a woman and she's been incarcerated for 16 years and still fighting for it. I don't wanna lose my family. I'm gonna be this homeless person again and I don't wanna be a homeless person anymore. I guess losing him, losing his income, and losing his family, I feel like I'm not gonna get that support anymore, I feel like I was gonna be this lonely, single mother of 4.5 kids. And then I would lose Juju, his daughter. She would be sent to her mom in Texas and we wouldn't be able to see each other anymore, and then her siblings.

Do you feel like that sense of family brought you hope?

When we first got together, me and Roeun, I fought for Juju to stay with us. And now I'm fighting for *him* to stay with us. It's like I'm forever fighting to keep our family together. When will this end?

And at least, for now, it feels like it ended, right?

It feels 90% done. Until we get a citizenship stamp on my table then I can say we're done. That will be the biggest party of my life!

What do you want for people who are going through or are gonna go through the same experience as you?

Not to give up. I know that sometimes it can separate you mentally, but if you can try to put that all behind you and just keep going, there is a light somewhere. I didn't give up because I believed that no matter where he is, he is still living, and we'll still be together. I don't know... Just not to give up. There's so many people here supporting. I did not realize how many Khmer people are really out there doing positive things until I met you guys. There's a lot of people supporting, and I'm gonna be there to support them too: the wives, the children, the family members. That's all I wanna do.

Bike Work as Self Work:
An Interview With Ke Lam

Tell us a little about who you are and how you came to work at APSC.

I was born in Vietnam. Me and my family fled the country when I was about 2 years old because of the communist party. Ethnically I'm Chinese. The town that I was in, Haiphong, it was a lot of Chinese people there. My family and I, we fled by boat. We were stranded in the South China Sea for 6 months before we were rescued by some fishermen, or in exchange for all the gold and jewelry and anything of value. We stayed at a refugee camp for two years before we were granted visas to come to the U.S.

When we finally settled down in San Francisco, where we lived all over the city. Lived in Chinatown, Hunter's Point, lived in the Tenderloin, Potrero Hill, lived in the Sunset. We just moved everywhere, wherever we could find housing. Around the age of 6, my parents separated. My brother ended up leaving with my dad, and I ended up staying with my mom. I remember we moved in a really rough, poor, Black neighborhood in Potrero Hill. Where I encountered a lot of bullying, racism, and also where I became a parent to one of my brothers, the third oldest. I stayed home for a whole year to raise him. I did whatever it took to take care of him, because my mom was never around, and my dad.

We moved from San Francisco to Richmond, where I learned about gangs. My first encounter with gang members, not just gangs per say, but Asian gangs. What attracted me to the Asian gangs were that, y'know, they're situation and my situation were very similar. Even though they were different ethnicities, like Mien, Hmong, Lao, but we had the same immigration story. How we came to the U.S., how our families struggled, how we got bullied, and from being bullied, they made a gang. At the age of 16, that's when I got jumped in, into

152

the gang. At the age of 17, that's when I committed my crime. I was sentenced to 27 years to life for a gang related murder.

Describe your bike giveaways, how did this program begin? Is there any connection to anything you shared from your childhood? What do you enjoy most about it?

When I came home, I had no transportation whatsoever, so bike was the only route for me. Bike and public transportation. Bike and BART. I remember when I got home, I was living in Concord, and to walk to the BART station was an hour. So a buddy of mine, Rudy Corpuz from United Playaz gave me a bike. And from riding that bike, it took me a week to really lay out my route to the BART Station and back. [laughs] But instead of the hour walk, I was able to get to BART within like 12 minutes. And so that was a blessing. Man, I see how beneficial it was for me to have a bike. A lot of people come home and have the same situation. They have no mode of transportation, no ID, nothing to get a car. And a car is too expensive because you have insurance and everything. For a lot of folks that were coming home that was a youth offender, like, we had no line of credit. So I said, "what's the best way to stay in shape and also to get around mobile?" It was to give bikes.

I remember I went to one of my friend's shop, one of my friends took me to his brother-in-law, his cousin, right. I said, "what is that?" Y'know, it was a big warehouse full of different people, and in there, there was a bike shop. I was curious and walked down there and there was this woman named Tiff Mueller and I introduced myself, "Hey, I'm Ke, I just came home, I'm just interested in what you got."
She said, "Yeah, we're a bike recycling place where we get old bikes, and we fix them up and we give them away and we sell them."

I was like, "Oh that is sweet, how can I get involved in that?"

Basically you can say, the rest is history. [laughs] We've been friends for the last almost four and a half years, me and her. Together, we donated over 600 bikes. I became very passionate about it because I've seen the joy in people getting a bike and riding them.

Can you describe what it's like for you, as a craft, to learn and to work on fixing up bikes and what that means to you in your life?

When I'm working on a bike, I lose track of time. Time is not even a factor in my mind. There's been times when I work on a bikes all the way to like 6 in the morning. From 11 to 6 in the morning. Not hungry, not thirsty. I totally zoom out. Each time I'm able to repair a certain part, if I was to spin the wheel and it's straight, to me that 's not only joy but a sense of accomplishment. I felt like, "Wow, I did something." And not only did I do something. Somebody else was going to be able to enjoy this, right. Whereas they don't have to pay the money, like most people do when they go to a bike shop just to get a regular tune up's almost $100. And for me to be able to give that gift to somebody, and then seeing their faces. I dropped so many bikes off, and I see the guys' eyes light up as soon as I open the back of my truck and say "Here's some bikes for ya."

Sometimes it took me 3 bikes to make 1 bike, and taking a bike apart feels like a stress reliever, like demolition. I was able to destroy, get rid of stuff, destroy stuff. [laughs] The other part was like the creation of it. Being able to build a bike from basically just a frame to a really functional, nice bike. I gave a couple guys bikes that, in the store, if they bought them even used would cost like $600. To give it to them for free and with no strings attached. To have the support of APSC and to say, "Hey, you need some materials? We support you in that." I was like "Heck yeah, that's cool." And even like carving out time from my work schedule to be able to give bikes away. I felt supported a lot in that sense because this was something I became very passionate about because it was such a stress reliever, too, to be able to dig into this, into this kind of work.

Can you describe working on bikes in relation to -- you talked about as a stress reliever -- is it healing for you? Is it actually something that you find has been part of your healing process in reentry?

When I think about healing, I think about challenging moments. Not just the great moments, like "Oh yeah, I'm into it, everything is working great." I think part of being healing is going through those hard times. Healing is those spots where we don't think about, that we need work on, or parts that we never thought would affect us. So working on a bike, brings some of that stuff out.

Oh shoot, I'm not just working on a bike, I'm also working on myself. There's a perspective, right? Because this bike is making me look at things that I either forgot or suppressed, or just never thought about, never knew I had an issue with. Working on a bike brings some of those stuff out. When I get into that zone, all these factors just come in play.

Me & My Brother
Maria "Kanaka" Luna

Growing up, I was my brother's keeper. I was five years old when my brother was three and he got really sick. My mom was working two jobs, and it became my responsibility to take care of my brother. At the time, Mom couldn't afford medicine, so she taught me Filipino home remedies. Everything had ginger in it, ugh. It worked temporarily, but I couldn't watch my brother get sicker. He looked half dead, and he was so sick that he was too tired to cry. All he did was shake and sleep. I took it upon myself to go to Safeway and steal a bottle of Flintstones vitamins and Tylenol cough and flu medicine for kids. I gave him one vitamin and a spoonful of Tylenol in the morning and at night. I couldn't read well, so I copied what I saw on TV for instructions. He got better in two days.

In August 1996, my mom, dad, and brother came to visit me in prison, and it was truly an emotional moment for everyone.

"Kanaka, I smoke weed now," my brother told me.

I shook my head, and then we both went out onto the patio.

He kept staring at me, puzzled. "Are you ok here?"

I laughed and told him, "Of course."

He got teary-eyed. "I wish you were home."

"What's wrong, Roy?"

"Nothing I can't deal with, I just hope you win your appeal. I didn't realize how much I loved you."

"I'm not dead, Roy."

"You doing this life sentence isn't living either."

I hugged him and told him everything would be ok. He smiled and started telling me about his girlfriend. We laughed, and he told me about the family gossip, and we shared a meal with our parents and ate. When it was time for all of them to leave, my brother didn't want to go. I held my tears in because I always felt I had to be strong for the both of us.

My family used to visit me in prison every weekend from late 1996 through late 2003. Then it became monthly, then just on holidays, until it was only once a year. Throughout the years it was very difficult for my brother to come visit me because he didn't have transportation, plus he started going to college. Time, money, and distance played a huge part in our infrequent visits. He told me on the phone a few times he felt like I was a ghost and he couldn't bear not seeing me. It didn't help when I lost my visitation privileges due to my criminal activities. Me and my brother's relationship just stood still—not fading, but also not growing. I didn't realize the negative impact this had on him as well as the rest of my family.

I didn't want to feel the emptiness and sadness, so I stayed in survival mode for years, suppressing any emotions that made me feel vulnerable. I transferred to Central California Women's Facility (CCWF) in late December 2012, and then I transferred to California Institution for Women (CIW) in April 2015. It really didn't matter where I transferred to or how close the prison was to my family, because I shut them out before I ever got incarcerated. I never meant to shut my brother out. He got caught in the crossfire. The only way I could survive prison was not having a conscience, which meant turning off my feelings as if I wasn't human.

It's 2021, and I am no longer incarcerated. My hope is for me and my brother to get to know each other as adults. I pray we can develop a close relationship and heal our wounds of separation as well as our childhood trauma. This chapter of my life is at a standstill, and I'm unsure if I will be able to write about it. Why? My brother treats me as if I'm still a ghost, so I just reminisce about old memories. I'm on the verge of starting over as if my old life, including my old family, never existed. But maybe one day forgiveness will penetrate through our resentments towards ourselves and each other—just maybe.

"The truth is that no matter what happened in the past, it is in the past. What I have is a choice about what I can do in my present and my future."

— *Eusebio Gonzalez, Letter to Abuela*

HOME

Art by
Kinson Her

Longing for Home…
Ung Bang

Our history etched onto the bones
Of the ancient asaras[19] - serpent demons,
Who guard the descendants of
Warrior kings - sons of heaven.

Ruling a kingdom
In the middle of our universe.
Many dynasties have come,
Only to perish…conquered…

Blood, traditions, ancestors
Forever forgotten…
Its people enslaved and abandoned
To wander aimlessly.
Longing for home…

But there is no more home,
Only the coming of a tortured death.
Humiliated and shamed
To forever drown in Samsara[20],
Heart broken and full of pity.

---

19 Asaras: also known as Asuras, are a class of beings in Indian religions. They are described as power-seeking clans related to the more benevolent Devas (also known as Suras) in Hinduism. In its Buddhist context, the word is sometimes translated "titan", "demigod", or "antigod". (Wikipedia)

20 Samsara: Samsara is a Sanskrit/Pali word that means "world". It is also the concept of rebirth and "cyclicality of all life, matter, existence". In short, it is the cycle of death and rebirth. (Wikipedia)

Varja pranas[21] and asaras
Adorn our temples,
Gateways to our ancestors, our blood...

My birth son - born to the fire serpents.
Our temples have always been with you,
Always in your heart's heart.
You have longed for home,
But home has always been with and within you.

My father, before his death repeated this story
To me. Passed down from generations to generations
As my father had always done so for me,
When I was a child.

Ungrateful I was then
For my parents', my ancestors'
And my peoples' struggles.
Their fight, sacrifices, and honorable deaths
To continue on heaven's mighty mandate.

I have never been more wrong in my life.
For I selfishly chose to humiliate myself,
To forget who I am.
I wanted to fit into their world, their culture.
What culture was it that they have again?
I look around me and see them
Desperately trying to hang on to mine.

---

21 Varja Pranas: also known as, Vajra and Purana separately. Vajra is a ritual weapon symbolizing the properties of a diamond (indestructibility) and a thunderbolt (irresistible force). (Wikipedia) Purana is a vast genre of Indian literature about a wide range of topics, particularly about legends and other traditional lore. The Puranas are known for the intricate layers of symbolism depicted within their stories. (Wikipedia)

My ancestors in answering my prayers,
      My longing for home…
Their messages I receive in everything
Around me that reminds me of
      Who I am…
My heart's heart… My journey home…

Motherland
Bao Vu Nguyen

Her domain is where the gentle mist
  casts its essence upon the dark fertile soil,
  while its milky cloaks swaddle lusty vegetables.
  The emerald palms of the coffee trees
  and the tender lobes of the tea shrubs
  are not neglected by its crisp embrace.
  The golden day lilies and the russet hibiscus
  quicken from their peaceful reveries
  at the fresh caresses.
  The evanescent mist leaves behind
  droplets like footprints that twinkle in the sun.
Her love trickles down on the budding shoots.

The regal mountains, soaring above satin clouds,
  are her verdant crowns.
  Arrayed in acacia and eucalyptus,
  their sturdy feet set firmly on her bosom
  while rugged shoulders brace the sapphire dome.

Down her valleys thrust the crimson rivers,
  pumping life into the veined deltas.
  Pikes, loaches, carps: silver blades of lights pulsing
  in the flow.

Rice grass springs in her silty womb,
  laden with pearly grains.
  The ample swords of limber stems ripple

like a green ocean from the flatland
to the stepped mountains.

Banyan trees, rooted to the bloomy bowel,
welcome visitors into their leafy arms.
Their knotty legs and gnarly limbs are
firmly embedded in the ground.

The rustle of bamboo groves in the breeze
answers the call of the thrushes and meadowlarks.
The canopies, with leaves like jade shards,
flirt with the songbirds.
Quiescent water buffaloes loaf below.

Thatched huts lull on rustic plains
as placid koi ponds stretch like open skies.

For My People
Michael Manjeet Singh

I'm what's called an "Other" 4 real
Cause in prison, behind these walls, that's the deal
When U R not black, white or brown
We (Others) got the smallest, tightest car (racial group) in this town
I speak my native tongue, Hindi and Punjabi
I love all my Indian food - especially chicken tandoori
When I say (Indian), it's not feather, but real 22 karat gold
And red dots, turbans and saris - a beautiful sight to behold
When I speak with my lovingly tight family
Only we understand our talk, so great 2 have privacy
We are a loving and loyal nuclear unit
When we pray, Indian-style is how we sit
After 9/11 (2001), racist times were abound and quite sad
Cause to be a genuine you (Punjabi) was seen as inviting the bad
But in spite of it all
We (Sikhs) stand mightily and tall
No matter who or where
There's always an Indian standing there
Ready to help after Hurricane Katrina or damaging storm
Cause for me and my people, to help others is our status quo, the norm
Culturally special events, the festival of lights - Diwali!
Wow! What a wondrous and special place to be!
Starting with the 5 K's[22] in store
My culture, I'm always hungry to learn more
The Kesh, Khanga, Kara, Kirpan
and Kachera, also music Bhangra and Bhajan
I'm trying 2 learn all about my history
So I can truly be the best of me

---

22 5 K's: In Sikhism, the Five Ks are items that Sikhs are to wear at all times. They are the Kesh
(uncut hair), Kangha (comb), Kara (iron/steel bracelet),

Formosa
Tien-Hsiang Mo

The chickens are anxious in their cages, their heads bobbing up and down, back and forth, waiting for their day of execution. The narrow street is lit with thousands of naked bulbs, strung up in crooked, zigzagging lines. The air is perfumed with the rich smell of oyster pancakes, called "oh ah jian." Oh, how I miss these unfamiliar sights—so foreign, yet so familiar all at once.

Taiwan, the Republic of China, once known to the Portuguese as "Formosa," is a tropical island populated by ex-mainlanders from China, tourists from the West, and native "Pai-Wan" mountain folks. Taiwan is my comfort when I'm in pain, my home when I'm lost, my hope when I'm desolate. When the corrections officers call for chow, I dream of the night markets, my cousins seated around a table laden with scallion pancakes and steaming bowls of handmade noodles. I wake up thinking about the muggy, tropical island weather versus this arid valley air I am confined in behind these brick walls. I miss the din and chaos with aunts, uncles, and cousins all speaking in unison. I miss getting bit by a thousand mosquitoes and sleeping on a bamboo mat (yes, it really does keep you cooler).

When porters sweep around the razor fences, I imagine Ah-mahs sweeping their storefronts, hawking betel nuts. As a corrections officer rides his tricycle up and down the yard, he morphs into a flash of a family of three on a single moped, weaving in and out of traffic. A plastic tray coming down the line filled with prison mush transforms into wafts of stinky tofu tickling my nose. These are the times when nostalgia overwhelms all my senses; ordinary, everyday activities in prison trigger my memories of Taiwan. It is how I carry on after being in prison for the past twenty years; I replace, imagine, and survive on memories of my homeland.

Formosa is the country I identify with; that is the country that whispers my name. Thirty-five years in the United States has only made me wish my next 35 years will be spent abroad. My name is Tien-Hsiang Mo, 牟天香, and I hope to see my beautiful island again.

Letter to Abuela
Eusebio Gonzalez

Hi, Abuela Juana, it's me, Sebio, your son. How have you been? Mamita, I hope from the bottom of my heart that you have no more worries, pain, or suffering, but are having lots of fun up there, mija. It has been so long since you and I last saw each other. To be exact, it was in November of 1999. I have to confess that for many years after my unexpected departure from you, I disregarded all the beautiful moments that you and I enjoyed together. Moreover, due to my incarceration in 2005, I never got the opportunity to hear your lovely voice again. It's something that I will always regret. Thus, Mom, I want to apologize for all the pain and suffering I callously inflicted upon you.

After finding out that you were no longer waiting for me, I felt sad, ashamed, and guilty for not doing and being enough for you. Since November of 2016, I have tried to shun my feelings over your death because it was so hard for me to believe and accept that you were gone, but to no avail. I've done my best during these years of my incarceration to wear a mask to hide my pain and suffering at not having you around to support me. This method of coping has been hard, and it is still impossible not to think about you. It's so complicated, Mom—I wish you could be with me and together we could revisit all the unforgettable moments that we shared. I want to believe that this letter is a dream, but it is not. It is reality, my reality, and you, my beloved mother, are no longer at home.

I remember that despite your busy life, despite all that you endured with your abusive and alcoholic husband, you always had time for me. Since the day my biological mother, your own daughter, left me behind, you took charge of me. I became your baby. Besides, I was your first grandchild! Although you didn't openly show it, you were so much fun, more than one could have bargained for, Mamita. Therefore, I want you to know, wherever you are, that I remember and I enjoyed every minute I spent with you, mi reina. Before learning about your unexpected departure, I visualized the many adventures that could make us happy. Now, however, it seems that I am gonna be solo in those explorations. Mamita, I want you to know that I admire your strong and outstanding personality, spirit, energy, and respectfulness, and the dignity with which you conducted yourself. One thing I want to applaud you for the most is that when Grandpa resorted to alcohol to deal with his vicious life, you became the head of our household and tried every possible way to keep your family together. This is true even though you were a woman and younger than your husband. You were the one who kept the family customs alive. I may never know the origin of your courage—perhaps you learned from your mother, whose husband was also an alcoholic. Regardless of its inception, you showed me, with your Spartan personality, that no man is needed to raise and care for a family.

In order to survive and succeed in that chaotic, surreal, and complex environment, many times you resorted to punching me in the face or on the nose so I would listen to you. Jefa, how could I ever forget the numbing weight of your palm? Especially the day when you hit me so hard that my nose bled, so bad that you couldn't find a way to stop the bleeding. It was funny afterwards. I miss you so much, Mamita. If you were still alive, mija, you would still be the strongest and happiest woman I've ever known. Now, since you are no longer with us, many of our relatives have gone bad, and as a result, some have walked into a destructive lifestyle and gone astray from what you expected of them.

Madre, I am deeply ashamed to be the one having to tell you that I am the biggest fool and the most naive of them all. In 2005, I got sentenced to 15 years to life for recklessly killing my victim[23] and for inflicting pain and suffering upon many others. I was driving under the influence of alcohol when I did this. Yes, Mom, I neglected your advice and words of wisdom when you encouraged me not to fall into that lifestyle of alcoholism. I realize now how ignorant and stupid I was. I thought alcohol would empower me, with the false and delusional sense of security that one feels under its influence. Si, Abuela, I drank in order to prove that I was somebody. Alcohol made me feel that I was tough and that

23 In prison, self-help groups often encourage participants to name the victim to acknowledge the person harmed versus generalizing by calling someone they have harmed as "victims", because by naming the victim, gives life and meaning to the person who was harmed. In the original work, the victim's name was written. To respect the privacy of the victim's family in this published text, we have anonymized the name.

no one could fuck with me. Without realizing it, I resorted to alcohol because I was hurt, and I developed a desire to behave violently. First, to maintain my overall well-being, and secondly, and most importantly, to defend and provide a safe environment for our family in any given circumstance. Nonetheless, I now understand that in my false illusion of being a tough man, I ended up hurting my people, killing someone, and traumatizing others beyond repair.

Sadly, Mom, it has been these atrocities that have offered me an opportunity to step back from life as usual and face life directly—to learn, to heal, and to take action to improve my life. Hermosa, rather than telling you how difficult these years of incarceration have been, I must confess to you that this time in prison has been, in a very strange way, a blessing. In this seemingly unlikely place of confinement, a place where degradation and fear are the norms, I found inner peace and a fortitude to reconnect with my true self. This insight came through years of hard work and with the help of many people who believed in my capacity to acquire an education. As a result, in 2014 I got my GED and graduated from numerous self-help programs. I am currently studying English at Patten University. Since day one, the professors have supported me in growing intellectually, emotionally, and spiritually without regret, while learning to cherish the positive experiences I had in my childhood as well as acknowledge the difficult parts of my past.

My teachers come from different backgrounds and different parts of the world, with a diverse range of belief systems, yet they have embraced me as part of their community and part of their family. Through their knowledge and teaching, they have guided me out of mental darkness. Moreover, they have given me something I didn't have as a child, an education. This is what has awakened the hope for myself and for humanity that I once had and then lost. Apparently, Mom, prison is not the end of the road for me—it is just the inception of a new perspective on life.

I know, my beloved mother, that this was not the way you wanted me to learn and to grow in life. If you were still alive, Mom, and if we knew about your disease ahead of time, perhaps you would take a special trip to visit me just to beat the crap out of me for being so stupid and for having done something so evil. Honestly, I would rather have that than losing you. I miss you so much,

Madre. I would choose wearing dentures, getting a black eye, or having you knock me out when I get back home rather than knowing that when I go home now, I won't find you.

I know, Mom, you would be very disappointed with me for what I have done. I did not live up to your expectations, and I did not heed your words of wisdom and encouragement. Nevertheless, even in your last moments of life, you could not help but be so concerned about my well-being that you gave specific details about what was and is for me. Thus, I want you to know that I love you, I miss you, and I will never forget you. I am sorry for all the pain, sorrow, and destruction I have inflicted upon the victim's family and our own family with my wrong decisions. I am sorry for all the pain you went through because of the kidney stones you suffered from. I am sorry for not being there during your last days of life. I am sorry for not being present at your hospital bed or at your funeral. I am sorry, Mamita, for not crying on the day you passed. I am sorry for having been so stupid and careless.

Mamita, I want to tell you also that aside from learning how to express my feelings with women and men that I have never met before, I have learned through introspection that to truly be a man, to forgive and be forgiven, I must let go of the poison of all my bitterness, let it gush out before God, myself, and others, in order to be free from my pain, wrongs, fears, and my old ignorant belief system.

The truth is that no matter what happened in the past, it is in the past. What I have is a choice about what I can do in my present and my future. In order to move on and abolish fear and loneliness, I must focus on the truth, and become willing to coexist without masks and without dwelling on the poor choices of my past. I have learned that being of service to others gives meaning to my life. Therefore, Mom, I am living a lifestyle in which I am awake, mindful, wise, and engaged in a daily practice of making smart decisions and responding with a positive attitude to whatever life throws in my path.

Madre, I don't know what the afterlife looks like, or whether I'll be seeing or hugging you again when my time comes to leave this earth. I have been a mean boy, and I am not sure if I am going to redeem myself enough in order to qualify to go where you are. One thing is for sure—that I am not going to see you or hug you when I get out of this place. I love you and I miss you so much. I am so grateful to you for all the love, protection, and nourishment that you gave me during your lifetime. I promise you to live the rest of my life honoring and respecting your memory and your legacy by loving, respecting, protecting, and caring for the woman that I am going to spend the rest of my life with.

With much love, respect, gratitude, and deep appreciation,

Your son,
Sebio Gonzalez
11/3/19

Fishing Trip: An Interview With Chanthon Bun and Trung Tong

While incarcerated we often dreamt of coming home and doing things we miss or never had a chance to experience. Sometimes we imagined what it's like and how it would feel. For years and even decades, I imagined fishing trips with my friends, despite knowing that it was a slim chance it would ever happen.

Now that I am finally free, some of the formerly incarcerated guys and I planned a fishing trip reunion.

Bun: Mr. Trung, we had a fishing day with some homies from prison. We got together. So tell me how that came about.

Trung: Well, I mean, Mr. Bun here, you've been setting up a couple fishing trips and you told me that it would be a good opportunity for all us to get together. And for some reason it happened. I started inviting all my friends at Solano. You started inviting all the guys in San Quentin. We all just saw it as a great opportunity to get together. You know it's been a while since -- a couple months since we been out here.

Bun: So tell me how we started planning. Was it like a quick planning? Or how was it? Tell me how everyone felt about it. Tell me about all the struggles you had to do to get ready on that day.

Trung: Ah man, yeah, I didn't realize that I would have to be the person planning everything. Like, "oh fishing trip," then bam, "what the hell? How come no one's planning anything?" There was definitely some struggles. I ended up having to get people into a group chat and asking, "are we going? Are we not going?" We had to find out the place. I asked my friend for some good fishing places and then I found out that we couldn't fish there because we didn't have fishing licenses, and it would've

175

been illegal. And then lucky we found out we could fish on the piers of San Francisco or something, but then once the day almost came, it was the time where there was smoke everywhere. The AQI was almost 300. And then on the day - we went on what, Saturday or Sunday?

Bun: Sunday.

Trung: Sunday and Friday was really bad but I don't know man you got some type of intuition guessing that the wind would blow it away or something and then it happened. On Sunday, there, got a lot better. There was still a lot of smoke but it was good enough for us to go. Yeah, it was a lot of headaches.

Bun: So had everybody fished before and what did you have to prepare yourself to go fishing?

Trung: I think we were a bunch of urban kids who never had any experience with this at all. "I did it in the boy scouts, but-" Um yeah, it was me and I invited my brothers and Kay. Then we went to Wal-Mart and went into the fishing section and was like, "What do we gotta buy?" Like, we all got fishing rods, but I didn't realize there's so many other things you gotta buy too! So that's why I had to ask you for what products I had to buy. So yeah, no experience at all with fishing.

Bun: So take me back to the day where we went to the pier and met everybody up. Take me to how it felt to have some of our friends around and see each other free and happy.

Trung: It was amazing, you know. I think we all felt the energy to realize, like damn, it was only a few months ago that literally almost all of us were in prison. It just happened to be that during this pandemic, many of us were able to be released. You know, Tith was released early. You were released early. Me and Kay were out there. Rachana, he was sent from Solano. He was released from ICE too. You know, and a couple other people. And one of the things I want to point out is the impact it had on my brother. My brother was the only person that wasn't incarcerated with us, and he was like, "Bro, I appreciate that so much because I had never gone out of that, my circle of friends, that lifestyle." And sorta just seeing us on the other side. Like we do have that experience of like messing up and doing harm to our communities, but my brother sees that for the most part, we aren't doing that anymore. Although we have that background experience, we're together for a different reason, and it doesn't have to be for that lifestyle. So that blew my brother's mind. Like, doing simple things like fishing with friends that we care about and just bonding through that. I know that it planted a seed in my brother's head to like some day I think it will bloom.

Bun: After the experience with that and the get-together and all that, why do you think for us APIs fishing is the go-to. Like, we gotta go fishing.

Trung: Oh man, I don't know. That's a hard question to ask. I don't really have a lot of fishin experiences but I have like Vietnamese friends, Cambodian friends - how they bond is fishing. I don't know. Is it like - I don't know - is it like a masculinity aspect that goes into it? Is it like a brotherly bond? You tell me! You're the one who is experienced.

Bun: Nah, you gotta read the newsletter for that. So the million dollar question is: who got the biggest fish and who won the bet?

Trung: Man, you know what, it was a big catch. It was a really big catch and everyone was happy. It was Dylan, and what, he's like ten years old? And he caught something and everyone ran towards it. The only other thing that was caught that day was a belt, an old belt that was caught in the bay. But we caught some crabs though but that's easy.

Bun: Looking back at this, having trips like this amongst our people coming home or even people who's been out for a while, been working, busting their ass, do you think these are one of the outing that would help rejuvenate and bring a lot of our community back together and have some fun?

Trung: Yeah definitely, even for me, like life comes and you gotta worry about your priorities, and I think like some other homies are in different cities. I think getting all of us that did that time together, that went through that experience together, is an opportunity to ground ourselves. Like yes, we're running with life, but there are things to ground ourselves, to realize that there are other important things too. We don't have to participate in capitalism because like really it's stressful right. The things that are meaningful to our lives can be hanging out. I think we've learned that in prison, to where we were able to slow down and focus on each other. I think getting together like that, even just once in a while, it's a reminder that we have that option. We don't have to be victims of capitalism and just feel like we have to catch up to other people. We already have everything. We have freedom.

Afterword
Eddy Zheng

Happy new breath, all my relations!

I see you.

I have been alive and free in the "free world" for sixteen years. Sweet sixteen. What a journey! While there is much to celebrate and be grateful for, it is still five years shorter than the time I was incarcerated in the modern-day slave plantation in the form of the Prison Industrial Complex.

I still remember the feeling of overwhelming love and joy at the homecoming celebration that my friends, supporters, family, and the Asian Prisoner Support Committee organized for me in March 2007. After being separated from my family and community for 21 years, the love I experienced in being welcomed home should be an experience for everyone coming home. Everyone incarcerated should receive the love they need to engage in reflection, education, rehabilitation, restorative justice, and healing.

It is also at this community celebration of my freedom that the Asian Prisoner Support Committee published, *Other: an Asian & Pacific Islander Prisoners' Anthology*. This is the labor of love from my ride and die Ben Wang and Sun-Hyung Lee, Joy Liu, Wayie Ly, Mike Cheng, Serena Huang, Helen Zia, Yuri Kochiyama, and those who volunteered their time to make a vision reality.
It was the first time in the United States of America that an anthology of writings and art was published by and for Asian American, Native Hawaiian, and Pacific Islanders (AANHPI) who are impacted by mass incarceration, deportation, and violence. That is the result of the model minority myth that perpetuated the ear-deafening silence in recognizing that AANHPIs are impacted by the criminal legal system and denied their humanity.

The creation of the *Other* anthology started with a longing to be humanized, wanting to be heard, inviting grace to learn from people who inflicted harm to identify the origin of their trauma, actively seeking love and healing through stories, and raising awareness to find hope and freedom. Since the publishing and distribution of thousands of copies of "Other," more people have learned about the detrimental effects of mass incarceration, detention and deportation, and violence in the AANHPI community.

There are more dialogues on policies and reform on the intersections of criminal justice, deportation, and the prison industrial complex. There are more directly impacted individuals, families, and communities coming together and participating in organizing and advocacy. There is an increase of resources to support those directly impacted and their leadership.

From being a grassroots and all volunteer organization, Asian Prisoner Support Committee has become a movement to end mass incarceration and deportation and a leader in the freedom of people.

Yet, with all that progress, AANHPIs are still lumped together as Others. People are still separated from their families by being punished twice through incarceration, detention, and deportation. Restorative justice and alternatives to incarceration strategies are seen as soft on crime. Prisons and punishments are seen as the only solution to public safety. Mental health and therapy remain a taboo topic. There is no call for systemic accountability. There is a lack of culturally competent strategies to support the healing and freedom of currently and formerly incarcerated people and families. There is minimal focus on disaggregated data on AANHPIs impacted by the criminal legal and deportation system. Pennies are given to organizations from the institution of philanthropy nationally. Internalized racism created gatekeepers to maintain the model minority status, decide who is deserving and undeserving, and perpetuates anti-blackness through fear mongering. There is little investment in practicing multi-racial solidarity.

Let's take a deep breath.

Sixteen years later, *ARRIVING: Freedom Writings from Asian and Pacific Islanders Behind and Beyond Bars*, continues the tradition of authentic storytelling to elevate the voices of some of the most vulnerable and invisible segments of the AANHPI community. Asian Prisoner Support Committee staff, volunteer community members, artists, writers, scholars, and allies remain the nucleus in following and supporting the lead of the directly impacted folks to nurture the creative process.

This anthology is arriving at a crucial time when anti-Blackness and anti-Asian violence are being used as a wedge by white supremacy and systemic racism to perpetuate collective harm. As the movement for Black Lives, women's rights, LGBTQ+ rights, immigrant rights, affirmative action, and our civil and human rights are under constant attack, these stories of courage and vulnerability are needed to help us find hope.

Arriving is the Ethnic Studies and Asian American Studies literature that we need to stimulate our critical thinking. It will allow us to activate our CHI – Culture, History, Identity. It is through connecting to each other's CHI that we are able to be in the process of healing intergenerational trauma and restore our original true selves. These stories are gifts that will help us find our humanity, our compassion, and our healing.

"Each time we take a breath, we have to give something back," a Native American elder shared with me many years ago. Let's take a collective breath and share the wealth of knowledge from the lived experiences of those credible messengers in *Arriving*.

I see you – let's get free.

Eddy Zheng
Co-editor of *Other: an Asian & Pacific Islander Prisoners' Anthology*

182

Acknowledgements

This anthology is a reflection of our community. From our contributors, to our community editors, to the many others who supported this project, it was truly a collective effort. From its previous departure, "Other: an Asian & Pacific Islander Prisoner's Anthology" (2007), this anthology continues the work of Eddy Zheng and Asian Prisoner Support Committee in documenting the ongoing issue of incarceration and deportation in the API community. Through themes of war, memory, stories within prison, stories beyond prison, healing, and home, this anthology explores the intricacies and nuances of being API and being incarcerated.

Highlighted in this anthology are essays, vignettes, poems, interviews, and art — all of which humanize API prisoners and expose the harm the prison system has inflicted on API communities.

Thank you to the contributors of this anthology: Adamu Chan, Bao Vu Nguyen, Billy Gumabon, Chandra Kishor, Chanthon Bun, Charles Bula Joseph, Douglas Yim, Eusebio Gonzalez, Franklin Lee, Hieu "Rocky" Nguyen, Hung T. Ly, John Lam, John V. Apollo, Kamsan Suon, Kanaka Maria Luna, Kanley Souetpich, Ke Lam, Kenny Lee, Michael Manjeet Singh, Nou Phang Thao, Ny Nourn, Phoeun You, Remus James Langi, Rhummanee Hang, Ricky May, Saiyez Ahmed, Si Dang, Tautai Seumanu Jr., Tien N. Nguyen, Tien-Hsiang Mo, Ung Bang, and Vu Bui. Without your words and your truths, this anthology would not exist. We are a more whole and healed world because of you. Thank you for leaning in to the power of writing and thank you for gifting us with your stories.

To our chapter artists, Chanthon Bun, Havannah Tran, Gary Taylor, and Kinson Her: thank you for your art and for capturing the heart of our anthology through your visual work.

Thank you to the incredible dedication of our community mentor editors, Amy Zhang, Andrew Yeung, Angie Sijun Lou, Annie McClanahan, Annie Wong,

Christopher Fan, Dayna Mahannah, Elysha Chang, Frankie Oh, Hannah Bowman, Irene Hsu, Jan-Henry Gray, Jane Komori, Jasmine Gui, Joy Xiang, Kenji Liu, LuLing Osofsky, Mark Tseng-Putterman, Michelle Crowson, MT Vallarta, Nadia Awad, Nirvana Felix, River Ying Dandelion, So-yung Mott, Swati Khurana, Tamiko Beyer, and Tiana Nobile for guiding our contributors through their writing process with love, care, and compassion.

Deep gratitude to the Asian Prisoner Support Committee Anthology Team and Volunteers, including Ben Wang, Nate Tan, Shelley Kuang, John Lam, Nirvana Felix, Kia Wang, Kony Kim, Janie Chen, Sarah Zhang, and Meghana Ravikumar for their support in putting together this anthology.

Thank you to our literary partners, Karissa Chen and Kelley Still from Hyphen, Rachel Kuo and Lily Philpott from Asian American Writers' Workshop, and Jyothi Natarajan from Haymarket Books for your thought partnership and support throughout this project.

Thank you to Thi Bui, Eddy Zheng, Victoria Law, Mariame Kaba, and Michelle MiJung Kim for offering beautiful testimonials that capture the essence of this book.

Thank you to Don Aguillo for giving this anthology structure through his artistic design, layout, and cover illustration.

Special thank you to Professor Harvey Dong of Eastwind Books for your continuous support of our anthology.

Thank you to Heising-Simons Foundation, The California Endowment, The San Francisco Foundation, Y&H Soda Foundation, and other financial supporters for their generous investment in this project.

Most importantly, thank you, the readers, for holding these stories with compassion and care. We hope that this anthology inspires you into action in the fight for justice, equity, and collective liberation.

About the Contributors

Adamu Chan is a writer and Bay Area native who was incarcerated at San Quentin State Prison in 2019 when this piece was written. He uses his perspective and experience as a formerly incarcerated person as a lens to focus the reader's gaze on issues related to social justice. Adamu draws inspiration and energy from the work of James Baldwin, Audre Lorde, John Coltrane, and the arts movement of Adamu's time, hip hop.

Bao Vu Nguyen is 39 years old, from San Diego, CA. He is working on his college degree in Sociology and is hoping to write and publish works tackling social issues. His main goal is to serve his community, wherever that may be.

Billy Gumabon is from Tacoma, Washington. He currently serves as the president of the Asian Pacific Islander Cultural Awareness Group (APICAG) at Stafford Creek Corrections Center. APICAG promotes cultural awareness, education, leadership development, and community engagement around social injustice, healing, and the liberation of our communities. He is a writer, educator, and an anti-racist and a prison abolition organizer. #FreeThemAllWA

Chandra Kishor migrated to the United States in 1975 when he was 21 years old. He is an experienced and certified business manager who previously worked at First Data Resources, San Mateo Credit Union, San Mateo County Hospital, and the College Oaks Nursing and Rehabilitation Center. While incarcerated, Chandra completed many mentorship and self help programs and became an AA Facilitator. He is proud of his work mentoring young people who are struggling with addiction. Chandra was born in the Fiji Islands and has two adult children. (This bio was written by the Asian Prisoner Support Committee on behalf of Chandra)

Chanthon Bun is a 1.5 generation Khmer community member and a model of how we can transform the community by transforming ourselves. He was incarcerated for 23 years and is now a Reentry Coordinator at APSC. He is passionate about immigration work, supporting formerly incarcerated people in their reentry journeys, and freeing his community from ICE. A father of 3 boys, he loves drawing and fishing in his spare time.

Charles "Bula" Joseph brings with him the life experience of being incarcerated for 12 years, and detained by ICE in Mesa Verde for 11 months.

During his incarceration, the Native American Sweat Lodge was a big part of Charles' transformation. After being invited and permitted to participate in their sacred ceremony, Charles began to heal from the inside and uplift others by teaching music, art, cultural chants, and dances that were performed for events in the facility. Charles organized and performed concerts on the prison yard to boost morale and in the visiting room to create a pleasant environment. Charles was elected by his peers into the Men's Advisory Council that was tasked with maintaining peace in the facility and bringing grievances to the captain and warden.

While Charles was born and raised in a strict Catholic family, he identifies as a Rastafarian. His life journey in studies of people's belief has taught him that faith is essential, especially to have hope in dire times. Within incarceration, Charles has meditated with Buddhist brothers, fasted with Muslim brothers, been part of sacred ceremonies with Native American brothers, prayed in temple with Hindu brothers, celebrated with Sikh brothers, and led ceremony with Pacific Island brothers.

In the role as Spiritual Activist in Residence, Charles will bring his knowledge and journey of being impacted to deepen the faith-rooted organizing around issues of incarceration and immigration. Charles hopes to be a messenger for oneness, that all faiths are a branch of spirituality, like all rivers, lakes, oceans, and single puddles are all water.

Doug Yim was born in 1979 at Flushing hospital. The bay area is his home. He hopes to honor his victims' survivors by never returning to the behaviors of his past that harmed others. He likes to play chess, scrabble and do music. He hopes to be re-sentenced in 2024. Please keep him in your prayers. At the time of this writing, he is serving 75 years-to-life.

Eusebio Gonzalez was born in Michoacan Mexico. He was seven years of age when he came to the United States of America. Eusebio left a household afflicted by alcoholism and domestic abuse. He came to the US uneducated and full of hunger, fear, and shame due to his lack of knowledge of life. He lived for 20 years in the US, and got deported in 2019. He currently lives in Mexico.

Franklin Lee is a professional photographer, writer, and Lead Reporter/Media Technician for the Mule Creek Post in Ione, California. Born and raised in Northern California, he has a Bachelor's Degree in Psychology from the University of California, Santa Cruz, and certifications in Photography and Writing from the New York Institute, and American Sign Language from the Interpreter Training Program at Santa Rosa Junior College. Franklin Lee has over 20 years of experience in various California publications, including local newspapers and magazines, as a professional photographer. Franklin Lee currently resides in Ione, California.

Gary Taylor was born and raised in Southern California and had big dreams that did not include prison. He spent his first ten years questioning how he got here and participated in dozens of self-help

187

groups, and then facilitated them. Just before COVID-19, Gary began to explore art and music at a level he did not believe he was capable of. Gary could not believe how afraid he was to express such an important aspect of humanness. A magical world opened up to him that helped him with things like control, anger, loneliness, self-worth, and what it means to be the man he was meant to be. Gary recently winded down his last year of incarceration, and he is excited to take his art with him into an unknown future.

Havannah Tran is a Vietnamese-American illustrator/designer and anti-deportation organizer. Her work focuses on stopping direct transfers from California state prisons to immigrant detention. She currently organizes the APSC Literature Club, a book club operating out of the women's facilities in California. When she's not working to free them all, Havannah can be found cheering on the Los Angeles Lakers and stanning BTS. Find her at havannahtran.com.

Hieu "Rocky" Nguyen is 40 years old from San Jose, California. He enjoys eating, hanging out with good company, and playing video games, especially Age of Empires.

Hung T. Ly is currently pursuing his dream working in the film industry. Several months after his release, he interned at a mass media and entertainment company and secured a full-time position which prompted his relocation from Sacramento, California to Los Angeles. He has since discharged parole and is working on record expungement to remove barriers and to truly live a new life. Hung enjoys trying new food and new things and plans to explore the world by going on a cruise and vacationing in another country for the very first time. As Hung embarks on a new journey, he remains mindful of his roots and continues to learn about his history by visiting his hometown and reconnecting with loved ones. Hung credits his success to the unconditional support from family, friends, colleagues, and advocacy groups like the Asian Prisoner Support Committee (APSC) and API Rise.

188

John Lam is 35 years old, a first generation Chinese-American, born and raised in Sacramento, California. He is passionate about criminal justice reform and works with non-profits from the Bay Area and Southern California to assist formerly incarcerated people when reintegrating back into society. When he is not working, interning, or going to school, he can be found fishing, playing basketball, and chowing down the latest cuisine.

John V. Apollo, aka "Hawaiian John", is 80 years of age and a HalfBreed (he had a Hawaiian-Boríquàn dad and a Southern-Italiana mother). He was born in Hawai'i and came to America when he was 3 years of age. John was raised in the Spanish Harlem and Lil Italia in Brooklyn, N.Y. until he was 16 1/2 years of age.

Since that time, John has traveled a lot and been to 42 states, 3 countries, and did a short tour in the military in Southeast Asia. And now, John is presently incarcerated, going on 25 years on June 9, 2021, for a non-violent, third strike for a second degree bank robbery.

Kamsan Suon was born in Kampong Speu, Kampuchea. As a child he survived the Cambodian genocide. With the help of the Catholic Ministry, Kamsan and his family immigrated to America in 1981. He grew up living with two cultures, Cambodian and American. Kamsan lives by the Khmer proverb, "Fear not the future, weep not for the past." One day he hopes to enter the Buddhist monkhood to restore the honor of his family.

Kanley Souet-Pich is a proud Cambodian American, daughter of refugees who survived the Khmer Rouge genocide in Cambodia. She was raised in Oakland, California. During her childhood, her family faced many obstacles that resulted from poverty and an unsafe living environment. Kanley did not get the opportunity to graduate from high school and became a mother for the first time at the age of 19 years old. In 2019, her husband was incarcerated and detained by ICE. She then organized her community, with the support of loved ones and CERI, to help bring her husband home. Kanley took inspiration from the successful campaign for the release of her husband and is now our Project Manager of The New Light Program, which serves unjustly deported Cambodian Americans living in Cambodia and people at risk of deportation, those being released from incarceration, and those beginning re-entry. Kanley is also an Outreach Worker and Interpreter, and facilitator of our Punlu Setrei Khmer women's group, and serving her community at CERI. She has recently gotten her GED and will further pursue her education to become a social worker. In her free time, you will find Kanley at home with her family, growing traditional Cambodian herbs, knitting hats for the elderly, sewing, or fishing. Through both her professional and home life, Kanley strives to embody the change that she wants to see in her community and provide an abundant future for her family.

Nghiep "Ke" Lam is the Program and Facility Manager for Asian Prisoner Support Committee and a former juvenile lifer. He was incarcerated at the age of seventeen and served 23 years. He assists formerly incarcerated, i.e. API and "Stranded Deportees" with accessing resources (ID, Work Permit, Mentorship, etc.) in their transition back into society. He is also the Facility Manager to oversee the maintenance of the office. He is one of the Co-founder of the ROOTS program inside San Quentin State Prison. One of his passions is fixing bicycles and donating them to our system's impacted communities.

Kenny Lee is a devoted Christian, from Los Angeles, California. His sole purpose in life is to be of service to others; this is where he finds his true sense of joy and peace. One of his hopes is to use his writing as a beacon for those who are lost.

Kinson Her has been moved by impressionism in the last 7 years and has started to incorporate that style in many of his art. As an artist who is to some degree colorblind (Red/Green) he's always been intrigued by artists who use color in their art. This has inspired him to

190

use color as well. Exploring outside of the typical black/white prison art has allowed him to venture off into the professional art world and successfully showcasing some of my art in multiple galleries. Through art, he has raised tens of thousands of dollars for charity like cancer awareness and for the youth at risk. He really enjoys expressing himself on a blank canvas, but what he enjoys more is giving back to our community and making a positive impact. It is through art that made it possible for him to make a difference in my community.

Michael Manjeet Singh is from Berkeley, CA. Incarcerated at 21 (1996), he's achieved many certifications including Microsoft and Paralegal. He spends time reading, writing and helping inmates assert their legal rights, despite staff retaliation. He immensely loves his mom (Purinma) and dad (Taru) and brother (Steven); their love fuels him. He maintains his innocence.

Maria "Kanaka" Luna was born in the Philippines, raised in San Francisco, and has recently put down roots in Los Angeles. Maria juggles two jobs: by day, she works for Homeboy Industries and by night, she serves as a drug and alcohol counselor for incarcerated men. Cultural diversity and racial equality are two important things to Maria: she believes strongly in becoming the people that our ancestors have always wanted us to be. Maria is a proud member of the LGBTQ+ community and lives with her fiancée. She hopes to one day add a dog to their family.

Nou Phang Thao is the fourth eldest of 10 children. His family and friends call him Phang. They come from a long line of compassionate Hmong elders, traditions, and culture. Just like these surviving customs and values, Phang responds to a crisis and life obstacles by being reasonable, caring, and kind. It's through these nurturing life forces that he can grow and become mature. He is proud to be Hmong and share his culture with the world.

Ny Nourn is the Co-Director at APSC. Her relationship developed with APSC in 2017, while fighting deportation in ICE detention after serving 15 ½ years in prison. Immediately upon being released on bond in November of 2017, Ny became a volunteer member with APSC's anti-deportation team and a council member of APSC. As a directly impacted and formerly incarcerated domestic violence survivor, Ny also continues to share her personal experience and provide support for people in prisons and ICE detentions as an organizer with Survived and Punished California and member of the California Coalition with Women for Prisoners. Ny is honored and grateful to join APSC's team to continue the work to #FreeThemAll and keeping families together.

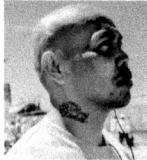

Phoeun You is 47 years old, born in Cambodia, and raised by forgiving parents. Being connected with nature keeps him grounded and at peace. He is empowered by being a student of life. One day, he hopes to travel the world and build schools in impoverished countries.

Remus James Langi is 38 years old. He is the first of his bloodline to be born and raised in the Bay Area, California. He loves his culture and heritage. He is the voice of his Ancestors through his simple acoustic storytelling music. Be on the lookout for the artist name "SkyBoii".

Rhummanee Hang (she/they/តា ត់) is an artist, community organizer, and culture keeper who was born and raised in Oakland, CA. Rhummanee's experience in racial equity work, youth development, and Southeast Asian anti-deportation organizing has spanned 2 decades. She has facilitated culturally specific programming for Oakland and Sacramento youth, grounded in ethnic studies and art activism. She earned a bachelor's degree in Sociology at UC Davis and a master's degree in International & Multicultural Education at the University of San Francisco. She serves as Co-Director at AYPAL, a leadership development, community organizing, and coalition-building organization that supports Asian Pacific Islander youth in Oakland. Rhummanee is also an Aquarian dragon, earring maker, and Mommy to the most awesome, Noreak!

Ricky May is 33 years old and was incarcerated at the age of 17 and was sentenced to 28 years. By the power of the people and universe, he was given a second chance at life and was resentenced. He served 16 years in prison. Ricky believes that life is amazing - the good, the bad, and the ugly - but no matter the circumstance, hope is what keeps him alive. This quote, "Hope sees the invisible, feels the intangible, achieves the impossible."

Saiyez Ahmed is 49 years old and has served more than 30 years in prison. While doing time, he has learned law, financial responsibilities, and investments. He one day hopes to teach people from the lower and middle class on how to do financials for the future.

Si Dang received his A.A. in Business and Certificate of Achievement in General Business from Coastline Community College in 2016. After nearly 25 years of incarceration, Si was granted parole and released from San Quentin State Prison in 2020. During his incarceration, Si facilitated multiple self-help programs including Restoring Our Original True Self (ROOTS), Criminal and Gang Anonymous (CGA), Juvenile Lifers Support Group (JLSG), and Kids Creating Awareness Together (Kid C.A.T.) as a way to give back to the community. Si is passionate about mentoring youth, volunteering with charitable organizations, advocating for social and criminal justice reform, and supporting immigration issues.

Tautai Seumanu Jr. has been incarcerated since he was 15, and he is now in his forties. Prison life has been suffocating him emotionally and mentally for a long time. But when he started writing, he felt air in his body and his mind started to breathe. It may be corny to some... but writing kept his crazy at bay. He is thankful to be part of this world.

Tien-Hsiang Mo would love to travel the world one day. There is so much she hasn't seen or experienced and a simple "bucket" is insufficient for her long list. She is at her best when surrounded by friends and family that she hopes to rejoin in the near future.

Tien N. Nguyen is 31 years old and has lived most of his pre-incarcerated life in the Bay Area of California. Currently, he works as an alcohol and drug counselor with the prison population, invoking change from within for people struggling with addiction and unhealthy behaviors. His dream of a world where people make connections through utilizing empathy and compassion motivates him to continue to share his experiences. He is a son, brother, uncle, friend, and mentor, but remove these labels and he is simply a human being just like you.

Ung Bang is 43 years old and lives in Los Angeles, CA. They are a seeker of all that is beautiful in this world. Their words to live by are: "Appreciate all and take no one and nothing for granted."

Vu Bui is a 36 year old life-termer. His passion is to one day earn his way back home and become a contributing member to his immediate family - as well as his extended human family. In his down time, you can find Vu either meditating in solidarity or otherwise goofing off with his friends.

About Asian Prisoner Support Committee

The mission of the Asian Prisoner Support Committee (APSC) is to provide direct support to Asian and Pacific Islander (API) prisoners and to raise awareness about the growing number of APIs being imprisoned, detained, and deported.

Since 2002, APSC has led programs in prisons, organized anti-deportation campaigns, provided resources to "lifers," and developed culturally relevant reentry programs. APSC grew out of the campaign to support the "San Quentin 3"—Eddy Zheng, Viet Mike Ngo, and Rico Riemedio. The San Quentin 3 advocated for Ethnic Studies at San Quentin and in retaliation by the prison administration—were sent to solitary confinement and transferred to different prisons. After spending months in solitary confinement (up to 11 months), Eddy, Mike, and Rico were released and eventually, all received parole (Eddy 2005, Rico 2007, Mike 2011).

For over a decade, APSC operated as an all-volunteer organization. In 2017, APSC hired its first paid staff employees and opened an office space in Oakland Chinatown. Today, APSC facilitates Ethnic Studies programs in prisons, provides community-based reentry services, and organizes deportation defense campaigns.

Contact us:
P.O. Box 1031, Oakland, CA 94604
info@asianprisonersupport.org
asianprisonersupport.org

Other Works by
Asian Prisoner Support Committee

Other: an Asian & Pacific Islander Prisoners' Anthology

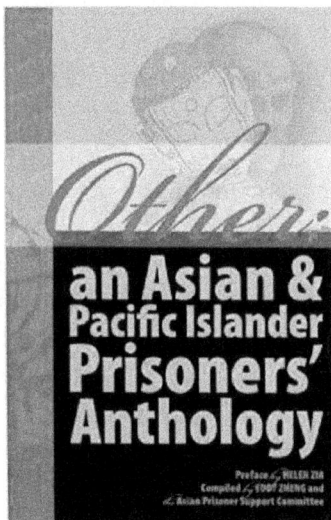

In 2007, Asian Prisoner Support Committee helped to compile, edit, and self-publish "Other: an Asian & Pacific Islander Prisoners' Anthology." This book has sold several thousand copies and has been taught in college classes across the nation in Ethnic Studies, Asian American Studies, and courses on the carceral system.

Praise for
Other: an Asian & Pacific Islander Prisoners' Anthology

"The writings are all so candid, real, different. They are so honest that it will amaze you."
Yuri Kochiyama, Human Rights Activist, 2007

"This has never been done before. These are voices that nobody has heard before, even within the API community. There is such a broad range of incredibly moving stories. You will read it and just be surprised by every page."
Helen Zia, KPFA Radio Interview May 2, 2007

www.ingramcontent.com/pod-product-compliance
Lightning Source LLC
Chambersburg PA
CBHW070108030426
42335CB00016B/2064